The Men who Made
the Settle-Carlisle

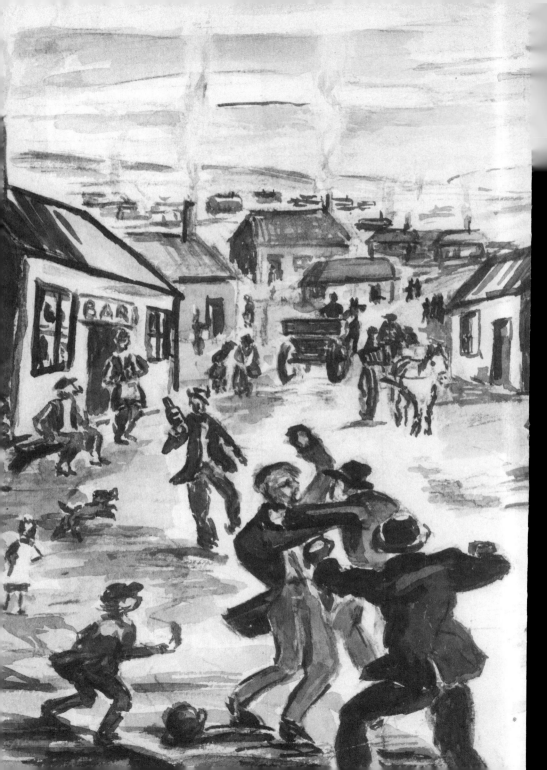

Settle-Carlisle Books by W.R. Mitchell:
THE LONG DRAG (published in 1962)
SEVEN YEARS HARD (with Nigel Mussett)
LIFE ON THE SETTLE-CARLISLE
MEN ON THE SETTLE-CARLISLE
SETTLE TO CARLISLE (with David Joy)
SETTLE-CARLISLE CENTENARY (with David Joy)
THE STORY OF RIBBLEHEAD VIADUCT
RIBBLEHEAD RE-BORN
THE RAILWAY SHANTIES
VARIOUS ILLUSTRATED BOOKLETS (with Peter Fox)

The Men who Made the Settle-Carlisle

by W R Mitchell

CASTLEBERG
1993

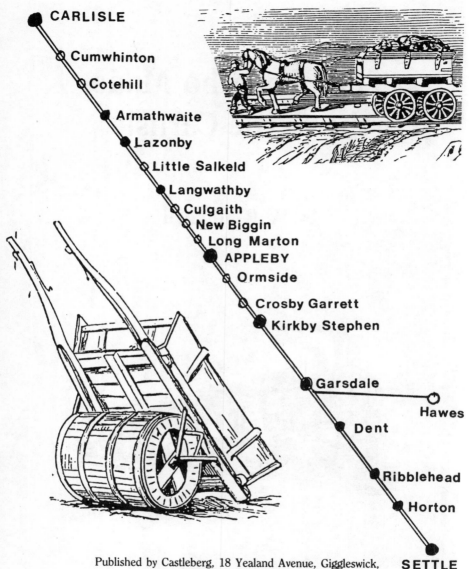

CARLISLE

Cumwhinton

Cotehill

Armathwaite

Lazonby

Little Salkeld

Langwathby

Culgaith

New Biggin

Long Marton

APPLEBY

Ormside

Crosby Garrett

Kirkby Stephen

Garsdale

Hawes

Dent

Ribblehead

Horton

SETTLE

Published by Castleberg, 18 Yealand Avenue, Giggleswick,
Settle, North Yorkshire, BD24 0AY

Typeset in Clearface and printed by Lamberts Printers,
Station Road, Settle, North Yorkshire, BD24 9AA

ISBN: 1 871064 86 4

Contents

Illustrations

Peter Fox — 5, 6, 52, 72, 87, 94-96, 99, 110. *Betty Harrington (courtesy of the Museum of North Craven Life, Settle)* — 2-3, 13-14, 34-35, 38, 118-119. *Rowland Lindup* — 7, 23, 47, 65, 83, 97. *Nigel Mussett* — 10. *F S Williams's railway books* — 1, 6 (top), 20, 53, 54-55, 57 (top), 60, 66-67, 107. *Sketch Maps* — Bob Swallow. *Sections of Midland Land Plan* — courtesy of British Rail.

Author's note

The Settle-Carlisle is not showing its age. The track is in good condition. Three million pounds have been spent on the waterproofing and restoration of Ribblehead viaduct. Denthead's imposing viaduct has been waterproofed and similar work at Dandry Mire is in prospect.

Appleby has a new water tower; Ribblehead a new northbound platform, with attendant waiting room; and Settle a splendid footbridge, painted in the old colours. Signal boxes have been re-painted and waiting rooms smartened up, with vases of flowers on some of the window ledges. Promotional material is attractive as well as useful. Proposals have been made for establishing an interpretation centre in the former station buildings at Ribblehead.

Sprinters maintain the regular passenger service. Special trains are not uncommon at week-ends and holidays, with "steam specials" bringing back some of the old time glamour.

The railway built at such cost of effort and money is now one of the best lines in the regions.

Whistles on the Wind

THE TOOT of a steam whistle could be heard almost hourly in the high fell country through which the Settle-Carlisle railway was laid. Now we must await the occasional "steam special" while rejoicing that diesel trains maintain a frequent service and carry half a million passengers a year.

My interest in navvies and shanty towns began over 40 years ago, when I saw a harmonium in the waiting room at Ribblehead station, on the Yorkshire Pennines. The room was still being used for Sunday worship. I discovered that in "navvy time", the 1870s, about 2,000 people lived in wooden huts that were grouped all the way from the road to the summit of Blea Moor. The Midland, anxious to pacify as well as Christianise its cosmopolitan labour force, appointed a Scripture Reader for the area; the contractor built him a mission room where services might take place.

At the nearby Salt Lake Cottages, I was shown a desk used when the workmen at Batty Green were being paid. Behind the wine store at Settle stood a wooden hut that was said to have been part of a "canteen" from Ribblehead, bought at the Midland Company's sale of unwanted material. It is possible the hut was once owned by Messrs Burgoyne and Cocks, shopkeepers and large-scale bakers. In conversation with the Preston family I heard of grandfather's role of nipper, or errand-boy for the railway engineers. He once took a message to Blea Moor and was allowed to descend a shaft to watch the miners at work.

In 1976, when the Settle-Carlisle celebrated its centenary, I was on a small committee formed to arrange for some celebrations. Nigel Mussett, Bill Brocklebank and myself researched the subject of the shanty towns to such good effect that we published a booklet and devised an exhibition.

By now, we were familiar with the shanties—with Batty Wife Hole, Sebastopol, Inkerman, Jericho, Jerusalem and Tunnel Huts. And we knew of some of the more outrageous characters, such as Welsh Nobby, The Pincer, Leeds Polly, Devon Sam, Tiger, Gipsy, Dagger and Belter.

My story is set mainly in "Navvy-time", between Ribblehead and Denthead, where the hutments were most densely packed.

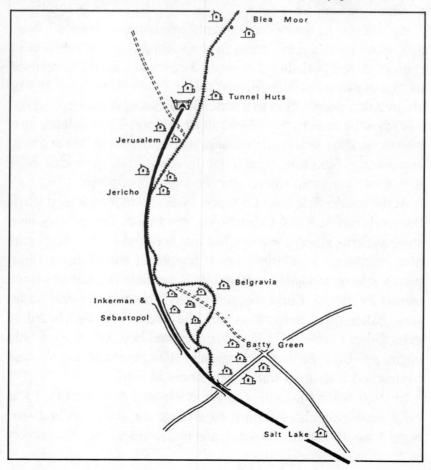

PART ONE

Life in the Shanties

IN THE autumn of 1869, the peace of Chapel-le-Dale was stirred by a traction engine which was hauling a four-wheeled van from Ingleton to Ribblehead. It was rumoured that the journey had begun in London. The van was brought to a halt beside the old turnpike between Lancaster and Richmond, near the place where it was joined by the Ribblesdale road. This is a wild spot. John Ruskin, travelling up the dale on a windy day, marvelled that the mountain Ingleborough could stand without rocking. The van, grandly known as The Contractor's Hotel, provided accommodation for engineers and their helpers.

The 1869-70 winter was long and severe and in the darkest weather a man stood at the door of the van and held up a bull's-eye lantern as a guide to his colleagues. The men who did the preliminary work on Blea Moor lived in tents and their supplies were delivered on the backs of donkeys.

By July, 1870, over 40 huts had been erected. The number grew steadily. The contractor soon realised that the large labour force would not be able to find lodgings in existing dwellings and so high priority was given to providing temporary accommodation. A typical hut was long enough to have three capacious sections, one as sleeping accommodation for the principal family, the second for the lodgers and the third to be used as a combined kitchen and dining area.

I have seen three photographs on which huts appear. One shows a group at Settle (in what is now Marshfield Road) near a recently completed viaduct, and—this being summer—the huts had been whitewashed to deflect the sun's glare. A second photograph, of

Ribblehead, with a partly completed viaduct, clearly shows a group of huts, some with porches, which I believe represents Belgravia, a rather posh suburb of Batty Green. A third picture is, I think, of Dent Head (the photographic image was reversed in the printing). It was here, north of Blea Moor, that a settlement called "Six Huttes" was established.

The style of the contractor's hut, expressing "fitness for purpose", changed little over the years, until the arrival of portacabin (for the office) and private caravans (accommodating the men).

In the 1870s, most of the huts were well-kept and had a homely atmosphere. "The hardy wives of railway operatives decorated their wooden walls with paper hangings and pictures cut from illustrated newspapers and periodicals", wrote a visitor to the Ribblehead group in 1872. "They make substantial meals, keep good fires and study the comfort of their lodgers".

In 1874, Sedbergh's Medical Officer of Health was appalled by the overcrowding and unhygenic conditions he found at Denthead, where some of the huts had been set on bogland. He estimated that the cubic space for each occupant in the sleeping apartments was very much below 300 feet, "the minimum required for the maintenance of health."

In one hut he noticed five bedsteads jammed so tightly together "that the sleepers, in reaching the furthest beds, must necessarily clamber over the others." The huts, being on boggy ground, were approached on planks or stepping stones. There was "no vestage of drainage save the open trenches cut around the walls of the huts to protect them from inundation." No provision appeared to have been made for the separation of the sexes.

The 1871 census is our first detailed record of those who were living at the shanties of Ingleton Fells, as the area was known administratively. The entry for James Tiplady is of special interest. He is described as "home missionary," having been appointed in deliberations between the Midland Railway and the Bradford City Mission, to minister to the railway workers and their families on Contract No.1. Tiplady's dwelling was No.3 Batty Wife Hole and he is stated to be 26 years of age. His hut appears to have been capacious, for he had a lodger, 21 year-old Jane Herbert, from Essex, and—to observe Victorian convention—a servant lass, 16 year-old Eliza E. Combs. It would be unthinkable that the missionary should live under a single roof with a young spinster!

Their neighbours were, by and large, decent folk. The men would return home after work, wash and tidy themselves, sit down to a good savoury meal, and then read or form themselves into choral or instrumental groups.

It was left to a Methodist local preacher to visit the navvies in the remoter hutments. In 1872, such a man, with the co-operation of the Contractor, Mr Ashwell, travelled by horse and trap from Batty Green to Dent Head. "While passing the numerous huts one could not but notice the pigs, ducks and hens wandering at large on the moor, showing that the railway operatives, however unfavourably circumstanced, cannot rest without they are surrounded with the domestic animals." Another writer mentioned an infestation of rats; they had "jovial doings among the hut inhabitants" and were "much given to nightly rompings above the ceilings."

It is known that pedlars made the rounds of the upper shanties and on Saturday afternoon, the Market Train conveyed shoppers in open trucks to visit the shops at Batty Green. A newspaper writer of 1871 noted: "Though the hut villages of Batty Green, Sebastopol and Jericho are upon a dreary moor far away from the busy marts of commercial men, still there is no lack of roast beef, savoury pastry, luscious fruits and beveridges of pleasant flavour to lovers of the bottle."

Overleaf: Artist's impression of the interior of a navvy's hut.

The name most familiar to shoppers in "navvy time" was that of Messrs Burgoyne and Cocks—a name that varied in its spelling—who served Contract No.1. The partners had premises in Settle and Batty Green. From here they supplied smaller shops at Stainforth, Helwith Bridge, Horton, Selside, Ashes, Sebastopol, Jericho, Tunnel Huts and Dent Head. So successful were the two businessmen that in 1871, within a year of commencing to supply the railway families with provisions, the partners moved to new premises in Duke Street, Settle. "This establishment is a great improvement to the street, and on this account the firm last week gave their customers 500 glass cream jugs and sugar basins."

At Settle, using two large ovens, Messrs Burgoyne and Cocks produced 4,000 loaves of bread daily and nearby was a large "butching shop" where four fat cows and from 10 to 15 sheep, besides "porklings and fat pigs" were slaughtered weekly. The partners also catered for the minds of its customers, and from the Batty Green premises were distributed newspapers and periodicals.

Mr. Cocks appears to have been the financial wizard. He pored over the books, and was quick to detect discrepancies, such as those occurring in the ledgers being kept by the manager at Helwith Bridge. Mr. Cocks immediately instructed his partner to investigate, and to ensure that no further goods were taken until legal proceedings began. Messrs Burgoyne and Cocks lost £16 of goods through a derailment on the light railway extending from Batty Green to Blea Moor. An accident occurred, the last wagon plunging into a gorge. Pilferers took the partners' goods—half a fat cow, a fat sheep and other merchandise. Incidentally, we know that John Clark Garlic was an innkeeper and grocer at Batty Green because a navvy called Thomas Jones stole an oil lamp and five pieces of scented soap from his shop window.

Food for the Mind

BY DECEMBER, 1870, a capacious mission room stood at Batty Green. The plainness of the walls was off-set by "pictorial embellishment" intended to teach the virtues of thrift and kindness. Across one end of the room was a platform, with a rostrum at which the missionary, Mr. Tiplady, might stand. Space was available for his gospel singers. The worshippers sat on forms with "backs" and the room was heated by large stoves. Mr. Tiplady impressed all by his assiduous labours and the Rev. W.M. Harper, of Chapel-le-Dale, was stated to be a man of genial spirit. In 1871, a wooden church was erected at Dent Head, to be served by Mr. Tiplady. Such a building was known as a "mission station" and clergymen and lay preachers were encouraged to take services here. The Methodists emulated John Wesley and in summer held open-air services.

Mr. Tiplady's mission room provided food for mind and body. In March, 1871, about 100 people attended a tea party. So much food was available that "large heaps of fragments were left." The idea of a day school at Batty Green was broached in August, 1870. It was opened in the springtime of 1871, when Miss Herbert of Nottingham had 43 scholars who were reported to be clean, neatly attired "and on account of their docility and good behaviour a credit to their parents and the railway public." Children from other shanty towns did not attend this school because of the distance they must walk and also on account of the poor state of the road. A visitor in October, 1871, noted that "groups of children here and there were sitting on the moor, which must, on account of its swampy condition, be very injurous to their health. Surely the

Midland Company might do something towards the education of those neglected children who through the circumstances of the workmen are deprived of the educational advantages of towns and villages."

It was at the school, in 1874, that a series of concerts took place to raise money for a tablet, to be placed in Chapel-le-Dale Church, "in remembrance of the poor workmen who have lost their lives by accident on the Settle-Carlisle railway." When it was announced that a concert would be followed by a grand ball, the demand was considerable and the dancers did not disperse until 6am. Another time, a concert was organised for the benefit of Leeds Infirmary; the seats were pricey but every seat was occupied. Messrs. Burgoyne and Cocks returned yet more of the good profits they were making on the sale of provisions: they sponsored this event.

In typical Victorian fashion, the Midland Railway and its Contractor did their best to divert the mens' attention from "pursuits and places of a corrupting character." As early as 1871, Penny Readings were being held each week at Batty Green where, in due course, a Reading Room was opened "for mental improvement and social entertainment." A Penny Reading included songs as well as recitations. The idea was to expose the audience to the gamut of emotion, from sadness to elation, by varying the tone of the items. The size of the audience was related to the weather! The proceeds were sent to a worthy cause, such as Leeds Infirmary.

Mr. Harper, the local clergyman, presided over an entertainment that was held in March, 1871; he "discharged his duties with much ability and in a goodly manner." Mr. Carr read "The Deceitful Lover" and Miss Ellis sang "The Ladder Stile." Then it was back to Mr. Carr for an amusing piece, the essence of which was conveyed in the long title—"Watering Milk, or Choking the Best Cow." Mr. Wildman rendered two songs and Mr. Tiplady spoke. Miss Ellis returned to sing "Barney O'Hea" and "Tapping at the

Garden Gate"— and so on until 10pm, for there were many en-cores. So often did the audience demand more from Mr. Wilman and Miss Ellis that they were kept going "like a barrel organ". A London visitor who attended the entertainment compared it favourably with anything he had seen in the "far city."

In the unlikely setting of a shanty town known as Jerusalem, where space for a public event must have been at a premium, the members of an audience watched with lower jaws drooping in astonishment as a workman carried a hurdy-gurdy about the room and played a polka, "which had a very exciting influence on some of the women, who could not keep their feet still." A contingent from Batty Green attended this concert and had to walk back along the tramway as far as Sebastopol, thence "by the nearest way" to their homes. The worst part of the journey was the cross-ing of the viaduct leading to the tunnel—a viaduct on which the train bearing the provisions had come to grief—for "there were openings between the sleepers wide enough for a corpulent boniface to drop through. Without a light, the danger would have been imminent. . ."

In December, 1871, a Reading Room was opened at Denthead, at the sole cost of the Midland, who agreed to maintain a supply of newspapers and periodicals. Mr. Duffy, manager of the works on the northern side of Blea Moor Tunnel, presided, being delighted to promote the welfare of the Mission and the Reading Room. Whereupon, the Batty Green Handbellringers closed the meeting with a merry peal.

Victoria etching of Ribblehead, complete with shanty settlement.

Law and Disorder

EDWARD TOWN travelled from South Wales to Ribblesdale, attracted by the 10s a day he might earn while working on the railway. In 1870, he made his home at Horton and then "wooed and won a fair lady amongst the hills of the north." In October of that year, Edward "led her to the altar at the lead-covered church at Horton." The quotations are from a newspaper account of the Welshman's dastardly deeds. He already had a wife and family when he wed the lass from the Dales. A message from his wife triggered off the events that led to his apprehension. On October 22, a telegram was received by Superintendent of Police Cockshott at Settle, and he forwarded it to Superintendent Exton of Ingleton. He contacted PC Goodison of Gearstones, who received it late on Sunday. The policeman had to wait until just after midnight before he could legally act; he then "pounced on his unsuspicious prey." The bigamist was taken under police escort to Swansea, where he faced his wife and family. It is related that his new "wife," on being separated from him, wept copiously and pledged that she would never forget him!

When Contract No. 1 was negotiated in 1869, the Contractor had to provide police cover as required by the local magistrate. Most of the shanties being on Ingleton Fells, the village of Ingleton had the strongest police presence—Superintendent William Exton, supported by Sergeant William Clapham. At Settle, Superintendent Copeland and PC Plowright (initially) manned the police station. In the "field" were Robert Walker (Horton-in-Ribblesdale), Robert Bold (Garsdale), George Renton (Lea Yeat), Archie Cameron (Batty Green) and John Otter Taylor (Denthead). The magistrates, local "big wigs", dealt out sentences with Victorian harshness and often sent a man to prison for a trivial matter. Newspapers were less inhibited than they are today and, for example, did not hesitate to use the words "rogue and vagabond" when a navvy called George Wilson was sentenced to a month in prison for being found in a barn at Dent Head with intent to commit a felony.

Court records are important not just as a catalogue of wrong-doing but because they give an insight into local life. George Morris, in 1870, stole some carpenter's tools from the grocery shop of Mr. Burgoyne at Batty Green. The tools belonged to a man who was doing work there and who subsequently met a man carrying one of the tools. He said it had been given to him by someone who was travelling towards Settle. There followed an exciting chase, the pursuers being the grocer and Mr. Burgoyne, occupying a horse-drawn trap. About two miles down the dale they caught up with George Morris, who had a jack plane—one of the missing items—in his hands. Morris actually asked for a lift to Settle. "Yes, jump in," said Mr. Burgoyne, who turned the horse and trap towards Batty Green and, on arriving at the shanty town, delivered

Morris and the jack plane to the police. Morris appeared at Ingleton Court and was sentenced to three months' imprisonment. One of the charges against Morris failed because the chief witness had absconded.

In the case of Policeman Jack (Atkins), the pugilist who delivered the blow that killed Nebby Scandalous one Sunday morning in 1874, the jury at the inquest, which was held at Skipton, returned a verdict of manslaughter against Jack, but no further action could be taken. He had decamped. To be fair to Jack, it had been Nebby who challenged him to a fight that ended after three punishing rounds with the collapse and death of Nebby. Perhaps he had not heard of Jack's record. Less than two years earlier, he had slain a man in fisticuffs and was sent to trial. Jack was then set at liberty—because it was considered he had not long to live.

The Sedbergh Bench sent convicted men to the Wakefield House of Correction, for Sedbergh was then a northern outpost of the West Riding of Yorkshire. In June, 1873, Henry Spring began a term of 21 days of imprisonment for stealing a cloth waistcoat belonging to Richard Bragg, who kept an inn at Denthead. A month later, at Sedbergh, Richard Tippet and John Mutton, navvies, each received a sentence of two months of imprisonment for stealing at Denthead one woollen handkerchief and one cotton handkerchief, value 3s, the property of George Gills, a miner of Denthead. They were alleged to have removed the handkerchiefs from a cabin at Black Moss, adjacent to the Rise Hill railway tunnel, which was then in course of excavation.

Elsewhere, a spade was stolen from Cragg Hill cutting at Horton-in-Ribblesdale and a counterpane from Jericho. Men who tampered with their sub-tickets (issued when they received an advance on their wages) were brought before the court with a wearying regularity. Among them was the aptly-named John Money, a miner at Blea Moor Tunnel. When he applied for 10s the sub-

ticket was given to him in the tunnel, yet the ticket produced in court had been made out for 40s. John was committed to the next Assizes, to be held in Leeds.

The few Irishmen among the workforce were exposed to bad feeling on the part of the Englishmen, who were not above threatening the hapless men from the Emerald Isle. Thomas Cooper, a stonemason employed by Mr. Duffy, a contractor for bridges, was with some pals in the Crown Inn at Settle on a summer evening in 1870 when he turned to a group of Irishmen and told them they would have to leave the area before noon on the following day. A disturbance took place. Peter Quin, foreman, was in another room; he came and tried to restore order but was struck twice in the face by Thomas Cooper. The police were called and "the row ceased." Cooper was fined 20s, with 12s costs.

Demon Drink

AN EXCISE OFFICER, John Barwise, pressed the Sedbergh Bench to impose a heavy penalty in a case where a man was accused of selling beer without a license "on account of the quantity of excisable liquour which is illegally sold by the hut-keepers on the new line of railway." A quaint name for strong drink was "John Barleycorn." It was generally recognised that the ale-can was responsible for most of the crimes. "Drink has been a gigantic hindrance," was one sorrowful comment. An outrageous example was when an inebriated navvy threw some dynamite charges on to the fire at Gearstones.

Temperance workers were concerned that two public houses, one of them being also a brewery, stood quite near the pay office at Batty Green. The Settle Temperance Society held meetings at which everyone was urged to "sign the pledge". Some did, at the time, while those who were shy of displaying their feelings in public later visited Mr. Tiplady, the railway missionary, and signed in private. A solitary voice raised against the temperance movement was heard to say that its supporters crammed everything down men's throats save drink!

James Mathers' "Welcome Home" at Batty Green was a licensed drinking place. Poor James died at Ingleton under the wheels of his wagon when trying to stop his bolting horse.

The "Junction Inn" at Garsdale became notorious for lawlessness under Emmanuel Brammall. Most hardened drinkers indulged themselves in private, frequenting one of the huts. The few excise officers skulked about the camps, peering in windows or, if they were not well-known, hoping when visiting a hut to be offered drink by someone who would then accept payment for it.

Drinking led to brawling, or even to pitched battles between rival groups. Two strong navvies who agreed to a bare-fisted fight had not been fighting long when one of the backers successfully appealed for the conflict to be postponed so that his man could sober up. The fight was re-commenced early next day—and was over by 5.30am. A navvy who had been drinking at the "Welcome Home" staggered forth and found the tramway was a relatively dry spot on which to sleep off his condition. The following morning, the recumbent man was decapitated by the first train. Peter Miles, a mason, drank hard and long at the "Railway Inn", at Batty Green. He set off for Sebastopol but was overtaken by fatigue and fell asleep on the tramway. The guard of an engine returning from Jericho told an inquest that when the engine was about 150 yards from Batty Green platform, a jerk was felt. He ordered the driver to stop the locomotive and found the body of Miles. The dead man was 30 years old and a native of Bootle.

The career of Emmanuel Bramall had more ups and downs than a Pennine road. Garsdale is a little to the north of the area that concerns us in this booklet, yet Emmanuel was such a character that his inclusion will add considerably to its authentic flavour. In 1870, he was a labourer who had hopes of entering the drinks trade. He was fined 30s for selling ale without a license. In many subsequent court cases, his name was spelt in various ways, which did not matter, for he was generally known as Nobby and was sometimes referred to as such. In February, 1873, Nobby was fined 20s with 13s costs for selling beer at the "Junction Inn" outside licensing hours. PC Bold found 18 men in the place; he watched the landlady bring in a quart of beer, which was paid for in his presence. Nobby unwisely obstructed PC Bold by holding a door and preventing the constable from passing through it. An additional fine of 1s was imposed, together with 8s 6d costs.

In June of the same year, PC Inman visited Nobby's premises at about 8.15am and discovered 16 or 17 men, several of whom were "the worse for drink". Nobby was subsequently fined for permitting drunkenness in the house. The notorious landlord had a wife with a roving eye. It eventually rested on a labourer called Samuel Seely, who lodged at the inn. She left Nobby in the autumn of 1874, and her husband went to Wales looking for her, leaving Seely in the house. When Nobby returned, Seely had gone and with him a black silk handkershief, a navvy's slop and a boy's suit of clothes. The man was tracked down in Fifeshire. The missing objects were in his possession. He had been living with Nobby's wife for three weeks, but by then she had left him and gone to North Shields. At the court hearing, to everyone's surprise, Seely was acquitted.

Nobby's career continued ingloriously almost to the end of "navvy time." In March, 1875, he was charged with an assault upon Elizabeth Thompson. He was at this time the owner of the "Junction Inn," with William Thompson as his tenant, Elizabeth being his daughter. She was fetching water for the use of the house when Nobby, without provocation, struck her on the eye. That was the tale told at Sedbergh Petty Sessions by William Thompson. The magistrates believed Nobby when he said that Thompson was drunk in the middle of the day and that he had turned out all the people including his daughter. He had given her a black eye two or three hours before the alleged assault took place. The case against Nobby was dismissed and so, whatever his faults, he was proved to be chivalrous towards a lady. The reporter attending Sedbergh Court noted that this lady was a "showily dressed girl"!

The Gearstones Inn, which stood beside the turnpike road near Ribblehead, secured a place in local folklore when young Sharland the engineer, and some of his men, stayed here while surveying the line. A sudden blizzard marooned them. Eventually they had to tunnel out of the inn so that they could obtain water from a trough. The enduring fame of Gearstones was ensured in May, 1873, when a railway labourer called George Young caused an explosion by tossing some caps and a portion of "Nobel's patent safety powder dynamite" on to the fire. The inn-keeper, Francis Yates, and his daughter Alice, were on the premises when Young arrived between 4pm and 5pm and demanded a drink. An hour later, Yates was seen to have a tin box in his hand. In the box were objects like gun caps, but longer.

Alice Yates heard him say that he would not strike one of the caps for a sovereign, or the house would be blown up. At about 7pm, her worst fears were realised when she heard a loud report and the house was so shaken by the blast she thought it would collapse. The kitchen and lobby filled with smoke. At the time of the explosion, there were 13 people in the house and seven in the kitchen where Yates had been drinking. At the court hearing, John Butcher related that he had seen Young take a tin box from his pocket; he removed something from the box—which Butcher had taken to be tobacco—and threw it on the fire. A loud explosion followed.

Yates left the house. Butcher, who was described as "a navvy on the tramp," followed him on to the road, "collared him and knocked him down." Butcher dragged the hapless man into the inn and stood guard over him until PC Cameron arrived. The accused was found to have 19s 6d, a tobacco box, a knife, a box of caps and a portion of Nobel's patent safety powder dynamite." He was committed to the Assizes. The damage to the inn was less serious than might be supposed. The oven and fireplace grate were blown out of their places, 15 panes of glass were broken, also part of a window frame and a clock. The blast shattered the glass in a framed funeral card.

Cases of illicit drinking came before the magistrates with a wearying monotony. One could understand the navvies in a bleak area like Blea Moor becoming hard drinkers, but cases were reported from the Lowland areas, too. In 1871, George Askell was fined £5 for selling beer without a licence in huts at Stainforth. Richard Buckle was fined £3.3s (also costs totalling £1.17s) for selling beer at Horton without troubling the Excise authorities. The market town of Settle had inns in abundance but navvies still found the back-street drinking places.

In March, 1874, Superintendent Copeland, of Settle Police, received a number of complaints about illicit drinking and he thus gave a pep-talk to his men, one of whom, PC Plowright, assumed a disguise and visited the home of John Duggan, a railway labourer living in Upper Settle. The policeman was served with a pint of beer and Duggan was handed sixpence and gave threepence back in change. At court, Duggan pleaded guilty and was sent to prison for three weeks. Thomas Smith, a labourer who lived at Stainforth, called at the "Royal Oak" in Settle, drank too much and appears to have mistaken the road when he left. He fell in the Ribble near King's Mill and was found drowned.

John Barwise and Joseph Wilson, the Excise officers for Sedbergh and Bentham respectively, were known to prowl around huts at night and, if they were not well-known in a locality, to enter a hut and ask for beer. One such hut entered by Wilson stood near the southern end of Blea Moor tunnel. James Oxendale, who lived in the Railway Huts at Dent Head, was fined 20s with costs for selling beer without a license, though evidence was given that the chief witness for the prosecution—a navvy named Pugh—had a grievance against Oxendale, having been turned out of his lodgings by Oxendale's wife.

The navvies must not be allowed to become too friendly with John Barleycorn.

Life and Death

THE FIRST AMBULANCE at Batty Green was horse-drawn, of course, and resembled one of the "covered wagons" made famous by their use on the plains of the American West. The Yorkshire type of wagon took patients to a temporary wooden structure. Alfred Johnson was admitted in a hurry on January 6, 1871. Alfred had damaged a leg while working in the cutting at Helwith Bridge and the leg was amputated below the knee by Drs. Green and Hartley. Money for medical attention came in part from a Settle and Carlisle Sick Fund, established among the work people towards the end of 1870, there being 140 members by the spring of 1873. A shortfall in funds was met by organising an entertainment in the Settle Music Hall, over £10 being raised.

When the Midland Railway Company took over Mr. Ashwell's Contract—he was in financial difficulty—they maintained their own doctor at a fine new hospital that was constructed at Batty Green. Dr. Swain, of Sedbergh, was summoned when there was an accident or ill-health at Dent Head.

Doctors were not themselves immune from misfortune. In the summer of 1871, during a thunderstorm, Dr. Griffiths set off from Batty Green to Ingleton, where his professional services were needed. A young man had been thrown from a horse, injuring his head. The doctor's horse, startled by a flash of lightning, reared up, the rider being thrown to the ground. Happily, he was able to remount and to resume his journey.

In its first year of operation, the narrow gauge railway from Batty Green to Blea Moor claimed several lives. Gloom descended on the shanty towns when the news spread of the death of Annie

Wall, aged 7. She had arrived at Ingleton station with her aunt, Mrs. Powell, and they travelled through Chapel-le-Dale and lodged at Sebastopol. Shortly before noon, the train journey began. Mr. Powell, having met his wife and their young relative, helped them into the wagons, Mrs. Powell and Annie occupying the first of three and Mr. Powell entering the last. Near Underhill's cutting, and not far short of a temporary bridge, the locomotive left the track. Annie was buried with muck and scalded by hot water from the boiler, Mrs. Powell being scalded about her legs. Her husband was uninjured. The driver of the locomotive suffered bruising. The fireman, who leapt off, was uninjured. At the inquest, the Coroner returned a verdict of "accidental death."

At an inquest held in October, 1870, into the death of a man at Pavilion Cottages, near the Stone House, in the upper valley of the Dee, the Coroner heard that George Hodge, aged 63, had fallen into a cellar being constructed to hold the stock of Mr. W.M. Boden, grocer and innkeeper. A verdict of accidental death was returned. Some men died of terrible injuries without the ministrations of a doctor, and one such was James Sherman, driver at Blea Moor Tunnel. He was bringing a horse-drawn wagon out of the tunnel one evening when he was knocked down. One of the wheels ran over his ankle, crushing it badly. Sherman was lifted on to a cart and conveyed to his lodgings at Batty Green, a journey of five miles. When his hut was reached, he had lost so much blood it was trickling from the back of the cart. Sherman refused medical help and died soon afterwards, the Coroner at the inquest returning a verdict of "Accidental death." John Lee, who fell off a wagon and went under the train on the tramway, lost his left arm and leg. He was taken to his lodgings at Sebastopol and died four hours later.

In February, 1873, one of the legs of a crane being used in Langcliffe cutting fell on young John Owen, who was instantly killed. The inquest verdict was "Accidental death" but the Coroner recommended that in future all cranes used on the line should undergo an inspection daily, by some competent person in the employ of the company. Owen's sorrowing mates attended the funeral at Settle parish church. A tombstone was raised to mark his grave. Following the inscription is a quotation in Welsh.

In the dusty recesses of Blea Moor Tunnel, in October, 1874, Henry Cartwright, aged 23, was at work when he was struck by some falling rock and died instantly. His body was reverently borne to the school at Dent Head and lay here until the inquest could be held. Miners had an almost cheerful disregard for safety measures connected with dynamite. Unexploded dynamite was left in holes in the rocks, when it should have been removed in case it was struck by a driller who did not know it was there. In May, 1874, John Roberts and Caleb James—the latter known as Birmingham Bill—were drilling when old dynamite exploded. Bill died soon afterwards; the other man lost an eye and had the sight in the other eye greatly impaired.

On another day, Henry Wright died when the drill he was using connected with some dynamite. Henry lingered for a while in Batty Green hospital. After the inquest, held at the "Welcome Home", many of his friends followed the coffin to the last resting place in Chapel-le-Dale. John Thompson was drying off dynamite at a brazier in Blea Moor Tunnel, one April day in 1875, when the dynamite exploded and he died instantly. Thompson was 28 years of age and his body was interred in the yard of Chapel-le-Dale.

In the spring and summer of 1871, smallpox was detected in the hutments on and around Batty Green. It was, according to a newpaper reporter, "painfully prevalent" at Sebastopol and Jericho. Five funerals of victims had been held in a single week, and from a single hut at Sebastopol were carried the bodies of a mother and three children. At a meeting held in the National

School at Ingleton, on March 22, 1871, consideration was given to the enlargement of the burial ground.

Meanwhile, when smallpox began to wreak "terrible havoc amongst the inhabitants at the new railway works on Blea Moor." The necessity of providing isolation facilities was an urgent consideration. At Batty Green, the contractor erected two huts for the accommodation of 10 patients. In due course, a covered way and another building 48 feet long, were provided. It was now possible to accommodate a total of 20 patients. Patients' clothes were "baked" in a large oven and all washing and disinfecting of garments were undertaken on the premises. The hospital was managed by Mr. and Mrs. Halifax.

By June, it was reported that no death had occurred at Batty Green for a fortnight, and that those who had caught the disease, having been removed to the hospital, were responding to medical attention and good nursing. They had "yielded to the remedies employed." Soon afterwards, an upsurge in the number of cases led to four more deaths—two of children at Jericho and two of men who had been moved to the hospital.

In July, the medical workers were disheartened by a resurgence of smallpox. The inhabitants of the shanty towns were being urged to be more hygienic. The interiors of yet more huts were whitewashed. At the hospital, washing and disinfecting were being done on the premises. A "dead house" awaited those who could not fight the disease, and the convalescents were provided with a small library. By July 10, 35 cases had been admitted to the hospital. Of these, 19 were cured and released and 13 remained.

Minimus, the pen-name of a local ratepayer, had little doubt about how to deal with the smallpox outbreak at Batty Green. He wrote to the *Lancaster Guardian* asserting that much of the trouble was caused by intemperance. Furthermore, all above the age of 14 should be vaccinated. "The ratepayers of the township in which Batty Green is situated should call a vestry and appoint an 'officer for the suppression of nuisances'." The remarks of Minimus were quietly and painstakingly answered by the Medical Officer, Edwin S. Green.

Many people had a dread of going near Batty Green during that smallpox summer, yet in July a party of Settle people went ahead with their plans to visit the dalehead railway works. A newspaper writer was impressed by the daring deeds of a young lady who, "with less fear than the rest and with a love for adventure, in spite of loving and fervent entreaties from her lady companions, mounted the locomotive and started on the tramway for the tunnel. This feat, which was considered too daring for the rest of the party, was only the prelude to further deeds of adventure. After being properly attired for the feat she had undertaken, she descended in succession the three shafts of the tunnel . . ."

A strange story concerning the Batty Green hospital was published in a local newspaper in 1874. After asserting that the navvy, when drunk, was not too fussy about his bed, and that this might consist of the roadside, the moor, a wet ditch—or a coffin— the newspaper reporter mentioned a visit to the navvy's hospital by some gentlemen who toured the wards with interest and then entered the "deadhouse." One of the party lifted the lid of a new coffin and was startled to find it was already occupied.

He reported there was a man in the coffin, whereupon another member of the party suggested the authorities had forgotten to bury him. "No," said the one who had lifted the lid. "He has his clothes on." The lid was lifted again and there lay a man, fully clothed, his trousers stained with blood. Had he been murdered? Had the murderer brought the body to this building by night, slipping it in the coffin? The visitors discussed the strange happening and concluded that the coroner must be informed. All this time

Overleaf: Artist's impression of a funeral procession at Chapel-le-Dale Church.

the "murdered" man lay face down in the coffin. A third man approached the coffin and pinched the man's left leg to feel whether it was rigid or flabby. The "corpse" raised his head and said: "Can't you let a poor fellow sleep quietly!"

The men helped him out of the coffin, telling the navvy he was lucky, and might well have been buried alive. The navvy, though still quite drunk, promptly asked for thruppence so that he might get another pint of beer. He did not seem particularly worried when he discovered the coffin was used for the reception of people suffering from smallpox and fevers. When his legs were steady, the navvy left Batty Green, travelling in the direction of Keighley.

An addition to the burial ground in Chapel-le-Dale was consecrated by Dr. Ryan, "vicar of Bradford, and lately a colonial bishop," on August 12, 1871. It was stated that 30 persons had been interred in the old yard since the smallpox epidemic began. On average, before the railway works began, there were two interments a year. Sixty interments had taken place during the past year. Earl Bective gave the land, and the farmers co-operated by donating land when a new stretch of road was required. The day of consecration was hot and sunny—perfect hay-making weather after a wet season—and the congregation was "as good as could be expected." The Rev. E. Smith had the spiritual supervision of the dale when the churchyard extension was consecrated.

Some curious tales were related of funerals at Chapel-le-Dale. Carrying a coffin from huts on Blea Moor could be hard and thirsty work, and on one occasion the bearers decided to have a drink at the "Hill Inn." For a time, the coffin was left in the road. The saddest story concerned the twin daughters of a miner living in the Tunnel Huts, Blea Moor; they died as infants in December, 1871. Notice of the funeral was given to the curate in charge of the parish in the absence of the Rev. E. Smith. The funeral cortege arrived about five minutes before the appointed time, which was

2pm. Yet no bell was heard tolling, neither were parson and sexton in sight. Then the parson made his appearance and told the bereaved parents he had forgotten about the funeral. Consequently, he had not instructed the sexton to make a grave. The sorrowing father borrowed some implements, dug a grave, tolled the bell and, when the short service was over, filled in the grave.

A visitor to Batty Green in the autumn of 1871 arrived just in time to see the funeral of a young man from Tunnel Huts. The coffin was taken to the tramway, where a locomotive and single wagon were ready to convey the body down to Batty Green. When Job Hirst, subcontractor on Ribblehead viaduct, died in December, 1872, a committee of workmen and others raised over £43 to purchase a tombstone with which to adorn his grave in the yard of Chapel-le-Dale Church.

Visiting Batty Green in 1873, and subsequently describing his experiences in "Chambers's Journal," a writer mentioned a man who could recall a good many deaths at the railway works—deaths from "accidents, low fevers, smallpox, and so on." He had buried "three o' my own." He was "arter a sort the undertaker o' the place. You passed the little church down at Chapel-le-Dale, near the head of the Valley. Well, in the three years, I've toted over a hundred of us down the hill to the little churchyard lying round the church. T'other day I had toted one poor fellow down—he were hale and hearty on Thursday, and on Tuesday he were dead o' eroinsipalis; and I says to the clerk as how I thought I had toted nigh on a hundred over the beck to Chapel-a-Dale. He goes, and has a look at his books, and comes out and says, says he: 'Joe, you've fetched to t'kirkyawd xackly a hundred and ten corps!' I knowed I warn't far out. They've had to add a piece on to t'church-yawd, for it were chock-full'."

When Henry Bachelor was buried here in 1875, it was said that this was the 210th interment. "Now there is some fear that it may have to be enlarged again," wrote the local correspondent. "Two hundred and ten funerals is almost as many, if not quite, as took place in the Chapelry in a hundred years previous to the commencement of the railway works. It is singular that in a mountainous district, so remote from the great centres of industry, men, women and children, from every county in England, as well as from Wales, Scotland and Ireland, should be buried in a quiet churchyard which few of them had heard of before they came into the district. Beneath the shadows of Ingleborough and Whernside, and in one of the loveliest glens in the north of England, many a wanderer from his home and friends has found a quiet resting-place."

An impression of the bustle at Batty Green
(the Ribblehead viaduct is in the distance).

PART TWO

Building the Line

WHEN THE Settle-Carlisle railway was opened in 1876, a writer in *The Westmorland Gazette* urged his readers to stand back and look at the structures. "The traveller over the line will miss some of its greatest beauties by his inability to see the bridges and viaducts on which it is carried . . . Nearly all these are remarkable for their great height; and, although they are extremely simple in design, the tapering upwards of their lofty piers adds a very pleasing elegance to their simplicity. They have all been designed by Mr. Crossley and constructed under his immediate superintendence."

Making the Settle-Carlisle also called for specialists in civil engineering and for equipment that was somewhat more complicated than a shovel. The Settle-Carlisle, being among the last of the great British railways to be built, could benefit from technological advances that had been made since the pioneering days of the 1840s.

This book was written for all who find delight in this bold Victorian concept and who enjoy visiting the bleak but attractive landscapes through which the trains operate. A visitor of the 1870s had a somewhat unusual view of a viaduct when he canoed in the Eden. He described one adventure in *The Field* in 1872: "I paddled towards the new viaduct of the Midland line to the south of Appleby. The buttresses of the viaduct were completed and I was loudly hailed: "Ye canna get through!" "Why not?" "T'water drops foor or foive feet." "But there's lots of it, isn't there?" "Oh aye, there's lots on it," came back his final reply, and pulling myself together I ran at my first weir; away shot the bow into the air, followed by a plunge, and in a moment I was careering down a rapid stream. . .''

Not all the devices used by the Victorian engineers were complex. One—the bog cart—was based on an idea that pre-dated railways. In Williams's history of the Midland Railway, published in 1877 (though dealing with Settle-Carlisle experiences in the previous year) we read: "At Settle, we stood in front of a 'machine' that consisted of a huge barrel, over which was a light cart-body and shafts, so arranged that as the horse pulled, the barrel would turn round underneath like a gigantic garden roller. . .'We used to fill it,' said our informant, 'with victuals, or clothes, or bricks, to send to the men at work on the line, across bogs where no wheels could go. I've often seen. . .three horses in a row pulling at that concern over the moss till they sank up to their middle, and had to be drawn out one at a time by their necks to save their lives'.''

Every story needs a hero. The Settle-Carlisle Railway has one readily at hand in J. S. Crossley, the Midland Railway Company's engineer-in-chief, who delayed his retirement so that he might supervise the building of this fell-top railway. When Mr. Allport, a top Midland man, retired, and a presentation was made to him of a painting of himself with Blea Moor in the background, he recalled: "Mr. Crossley and I went on a voyage of discovery—'prospecting'. We walked miles and miles; in fact, I think I may safely say, we walked over a greater part of the line from Settle to Carlisle, and we found it comparatively easy sailing till we got to that terrible place, Blea Moor. We spent an afternoon there looking at it. . .If I have had one work in my life that gave me more anxiety than another, it was this Settle and Carlisle line."

John Crossley had to oversee a major engineering project and send soothing reports to the Midland directors at Derby, to whom the project was a considerable drain on their financial resources in a difficult, inflationary period. On the Settle-Carlisle, things were never quite as they seemed. The aforementioned Mr. Williams recorded that in sinking the foundations of Smardale viaduct an unexpected difficulty appeared. The river seemed to be running clear immediately over the solid rock, which appeared to supply an excellent foundation.

"We began to sink," said the engineer, "but not a bit of rock was to be found. The limestone rock and the 'brockram' were gone; and we had to go down 45 feet through the clay till we came to the red shale, and upon it we built."

This story of railway-building is presented in five main sections, each representing the extent of a Contract awarded by the Midland. (The fifth Contract was for the Hawes branch). The initials following each note relate to the periodical in which it appeared; refer to the list of abbreviations for further details. The co-operation of British Railways in providing some contemporary documents is warmly acknowledged.

I have presented the quotations as they were originally written, which means there are variations in the spelling of place names and in punctuation.

M.R. (1876)

Initials in the text:

C.J.   — Chambers's Journal.
C.W.A.— Cumberland and Westmorland Advertiser.
L.G.   — Lancaster Guardian.
M.R.   — F.S. William's "Midland Railway" 1877.
W.A.   — Wildman's Almanac (Settle).
W.G.   — Westmorland Gazette.

Ribble to the Eden

THE LINE is now being constructed in Sectional Contracts, under the superindendence of—

John H. Crossley, Esq., as Engineer-in-Chief of the Midland Railway Co; John Thomson, Consulting Resident Engineer.

Contract No 1—Resident Engineers, R.E. Wilson and Edgar O. Ferguson; Contractor, John Ashwell; Contractor's Agents, James Hope, W.H.Ashwell. (The Contract No. 1 is now being carried on by the Midland Co., A. Terry being the agent assisted by W.H. Ashwell).

Contract No. 2—John S. Storey, Resident Engineer; Assistant Engineer, Frank Lynde; Contractors, Benton and Woodiwiss; Contractors' Agent, James Hay.

Contract No. 3—Resident Engineer, Jesse Drage; Contractor, Joseph Firbank; Contractor's Agent, J. Throstle.

Contract No. 4—Resident Engineers, John Allis and Samuel Paine; Contractor, John Bayliss; Contractor's Agents, J. Lambert, E. Williams.

Contract No. 5 (Hawes branch)—Resident Engineer, Edward Newcome; Contractors, Benton and Woodiwiss; Contractor's Agent, James Hay.

W.A. (1873)

A list of head and hand workers connected with railway making may be interesting to the curious. Directors, engineers-in-chief, resident engineers, contractors and sub-contractors, inspectors, clerks, cashiers, gangers, time-keepers, masons, brickmakers, masons' and brickmakers' labourers, carpenters, minders, platelayers, horsekeepers, carpenters, engine drivers, stokers, tippers, saddlers, mechanics, sawyers, quarrymen, cement burners, mortar grinders, engine tenters, and navvies. Lawyers and doctors have a share in the concern, but as one did not know which niche to give them, prudence directed a separate recognition.

L.G. (1873)

How easily in railway construction could money be wasted or spent to misuse if the head direction were faulty; for one day on this line if every man did work that was of no use we reckon the amount of wages alone would equal about £1,200. This is calculating 6,000 men at four shillings per diem.

W.A. (1874)

If the line had been simply a branch line, quicker curves and steeper gradients no doubt would have been adopted and a comparatively light line secured on the sidelong hills, twisting and twirling in and out to avoid cuttings and embankments; but the Settle to Carlisle is to be a trunk link on which the traffic will be of great dimensions and in this case flat curves and as good gradients as possible must be adopted. And when one thinks by the means of curves and inclines the number of routes that could be selected it shews a masterly mind to be able to conquer all the various obstacles and difficulties that retard the way.

W.A. (1874)

Contract No. 1:
Settle Junction to Dent Head

The Railway commences by a junction with the present line, 1½ miles south of Settle Station, 125 feet above sea level, where there are temporary sidings in connection with the tramway for the receipt of materials from the main line destined for the works.

W.A. (1873)

The junction of the new line with the *Little North Western* is at a point little short of two miles south of Settle, and at an elevation of 425 feet above sea level. The bridges between the junction and Settle are a skew girder bridge of 62 feet span, and an arched one of 39 feet span. They are of excellent material, are well finished, and to passers on the road they have a very neat appearance. No. 1 or Anley Cutting is a very long and deep excavation, through very hard grit, which proved very serviceable for bridges and other works of masonry. Many men were employed in dressing the batters with excellent soil, which gave the batters a garden-like apearance.

L.G. (1873)

At Settle we notice a large quantity of land enclosed, at present a busy scene of importance, occupied by temporary buildings, stables, sawing machine, mortar mill, etc. The mortar is composed of lime from Leicestershire known as "Hydraulic"; it is ground here by steam power, and carried in trucks to the various bridges.

W.A. (1873)

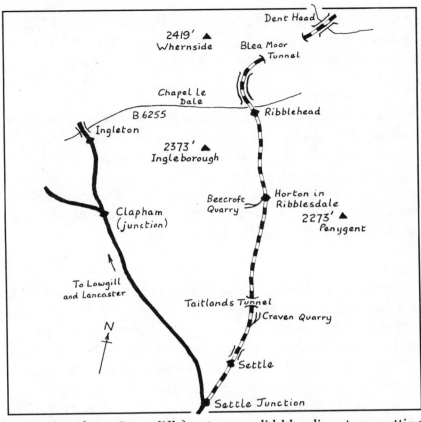

The line [near Langcliffe] enters a solid blue limestone cutting at the entrance of which a pretty light iron girder bridge is finished for the footpath leading from Langcliffe to Langcliffe Place and Mills: it is also spanned in two places by "fly-arches" which start from the solid rock and are about 42ft span. In this cutting are a few spar lodes charged slightly with copper, and we should think it looks a likely place for lead if a shaft was sunk to a greater depth.

W.A. (1874)

At Willy Wood or the "Stainforth Sidings", as it is called on the signal box, all the necessary sidings are in for the accommodation of the Craven Lime Company and Mr. Thomas Murgatroyd, both of which firms are sending off large quantities of Lime and Limestone, and they keep a great many men employed.

W.A. (1876)

Near Willy Wood, north of Langcliffe, the Craven Lime Company is erecting extensive limeworks on Hoffman's patent. The chimney, which is to be 204 feet in height, is more than half of its height, and as such a lofty brick structure needed a good foundation, it is built on chisled limestone six feet below the surface. Mr. George Dawson, of Leeds, is the contractor for the chimney, which will take about 200,000 bricks.

L.G. (1873)

Further on at Sherwood Brow a pretty peep is had of the Ribble and two handsome bridges are nearly finished over the river. This part of the line is an ingenious piece of engineering, the peculiarity of the district involving crossing the river twice. The first bridge is built to an angle of 34 degrees, and the wing walls are of great length, to prevent the embankment falling into the river.

W.A. (1873)

A mile beyond Stainforth we for the first time pass over the wide rocky bed of the Ribble by a three-arched bridge. Here the engineers had great difficulty in selecting the best route to be taken. Should they cross and re-cross the river, or by two very heavy cuttings, and perhaps tunnels, to take the line further to the east. The bridge is built at an angle of 34 degrees, and the long wing walls that sustain the embankment are of ingenious construction, though they were not liked by the builders on account of the number of "quoins" or corners they required.

M.R. (1876)

Elworth (Helwith) Bridge is a fine new structure seven yards wide, and is considerably higher than the old narrow bridge which is not yet taken down. Near this bridge, on the south side of the stream, a lucky workman just commencing business for himself, built a small sawmill for flags on the land through which the railway would run, but as he, in the multiplicity of business, had been overlooked, report says that he secured £700 as compensation.

L.G. (1873)

Helwith or Elworth Bridge is to be entirely rebuilt on a fresh site. The road has to be raised to enable the railway to pass underneath it, and involves a viaduct of five arches. The site of an ancient tarn has evidently been crossed by the line near here, as we are told the foundations of some of the bridges are twelve feet below the surface through silt and washings...The locomotive from Settle now runs as far as Row End for Horton.

W.A. (1873)

From Selside to Dent Head about 1,050 men are employed. Mr. Crossley, of Derby, is the engineer-in-chief. Mr. Wilson, of Settle, is resident engineer for No. 1 division of No. 1 contract; Mr E.O. Ferguson, resident engineer for No. 2 division of contract No. 1. Mr. A. Terry is chief agent for the company who now carry on the works of No. 1 contract, Mr. John Ashwell having given up his contract. Mr. W.H. Ashwell is agent or manager of the northern end of this contract, under Mr. Terry.

L.G. (1873)

At half a mile south of Selside the "pot hole" has been filled up and adds largely to the size of the field. The filling in this hole prevented all possibility of the embankment slipping. A tip waggon lies buried at the bottom as it accidentally slipped over, and it would have been more expense pulling it up than what it was worth.

W.A. (1876)

"I have known the men," remarked Mr. Crossley to us the other day, "blast the boulder-clay like rock and within a few hours have to ladle out the same stuff from the same spot like soup in buckets. Or a man strikes a blow with his pick at what he thinks is clay, but there is a great boulder underneath almost as hard as iron, and the man's wrists, arms and body are so shaken by the shock that, disgusted, he flings down his tools, asks for his money, and is off. . .

M.R. (1876)

One of the dwellings in this little wooden town is differently constructed from all the rest, as from its appearance, it must have served as a caravan. It was said that it was brought all the way from London, and that it was the first human dwelling fixed on Batty Green.

L.G. (1870)

After tea, Mr. Pollen entertained me with a historical account of Batty-wife-hole, from his first appearance in a van on its soil, exactly three years previous. Shortly afterwards, he said, "some chaps came down to make experimental borings, and they had to bide wi' us in the wan, for there were nowheres else to bide. All that winter there were ten of us living in that van, and a tight fit it were, surely. Of a night I used to have to stand by it for half an hour with a bull's-eye as a guide to the men homecoming through the waste. Sometimes one would stick, and his mates would have to dig him out; there were two chain o' knee-deep water four times a day for the fellows atween their meat and their work.

C.J. (1872)

Making one's way to Batty Green, one could not but look with astonishment at the numerous huts which dot the moor, and are known as Batty Green, Sebastopol, Jericho, Jerusalem and Tunnel huts. At the first mentioned place there are a mission room, day and Sunday Schools, a public library, post office, and shops for the sale of a variety of merchandise, a new and neat looking hospital with a covered walk for convalescent patients. All is life and bustle at this moorland town of huts, potters' carts, traps and horses for hire, drapers' carts, milk carts, green grocers' carts, butchers' carts, bakers' carts, and brewers' drays in addition to which may be seen numerous pedestrian hawkers plying from hut to hut their different trades. The company's offices, yard, stables, store rooms, shops etc. take up a large space of ground at Batty Green.

L.G. (1873)

The railway crosses the turnpike road to Ingleton [at Batty Green] by a handsome arch bridge, on the "skew", span 39 ft., in very massive masonry of blue limestone. We notice blocks of stone eight feet in length. One hundred yards from this bridge, towards the tunnel, an embankment is being tipped, which will contain 280,000 cubic yards of earth when finished. There still remains a large proportion of this to be done, although as much as 800 cubic yards can be "tipped" per day.

W.A. (1873)

The greatest quantity of men employed on Contract No. 1 is about 2,300 and about 130 horses.

W.A. (1873)

After taking some refreshment at Ingleton...the journey to Batty Green had to be performed on foot. Carts laden with coal and railway material were numerous, but there were no public conveyances for passengers...

L.G. (1871)

The population at Batty Green at the present date is from 250 to 300. It is here where all the operatives at Dent Head, Sebastopol, Batty Wife Hole and Selside are paid. It is said that last Saturday night their wages amounted to about £1,500. This was exclusive of "sub" money and the large sums paid to tradesmen and farmers and others who cart materials to the works. The number of men employed on the works between Batty Wife Hole and Dent Head is about 700. Upwards of 100 horses are also employed in this division of the contract.

L.G. (1870)

A tramway is being laid between Batty Wife Hole and the south end of the tunnel, which is at the distance of two and a half miles. This iron road, which will be a great saving of horse flesh, is within a few hundred yards of being completed. An engine of twelve-horse power is in daily use on this tramway.

L.G. (1870)

The brick-making establishment (at Batty Green) is under the management of Mr. Rixon. The brick works cover a large space of moorland and consist of extensive drying sheds, ovens, a large patent brick-making machine by Porter and Co., of Carlisle, a crushing machine, and a traveller seventy yards long to deliver the bricks in the shed above the ovens where they are dried by the waste heat. Porter's machine when in full work will make about 20,000 bricks a day. At present, as only half of it is at work, it makes from 11,000 to 12,000 a day. There are ten ovens with two fire holes to each oven. An oven holds from fourteen to fifteen thousand bricks, and it takes about a week to burn them. The quantity of fuel consumed at these works is only half the quantity used at an ordinary brick kiln.

The bed of clay which lies under a thin strata of peat is a mud deposit and much of it on account of its sandy nature is thrown aside. A crushing machine is employed to grind shale which, being intermixed with the clay used at the works, yields bricks of such a superior quality that when thrown out of the ovens they ring like pots. From 26 to 28 persons are employed at the works. Two girls were busy carrying bricks from the never-ceasing traveller. The large quantities of bricks made at these works are used for lining and arching the tunnel.

L.G. (1871)

Batty Moss Viaduct, is under the superintendence of Mr. Hurst. . . This immense structure, when finished, will consist of twenty-four arches, each arch of 45ft span and 18ft rise. The piers, which are being built of black marble dug out of a quarry on Mr. Farrer's estate, will terminate at springing with a thickness of 6ft, the batter on the face being 1 inch in 32. The north abutment and the piers for the first six openings are already raised to heights varying from 10 to 25ft. The foundations for the next six piers are put in and built up to the level. The foundations are taken down to solid rock, which is mountain limestone. . . The lime used at the works is Barrow lime, brought from the neighbourhood of Leicester. The limestone of which the viaduct is built burns to a very good hydraulic lime.

The staging for a quarter of the length of the viaduct is to the height of within 20 feet of springing. A steam crane is employed to unload the stone, and two hand cranes and their travellers to turn the stone and for setting it. The whole of the stone is brought from two quarries under Whernside, at the distance of one and a quarter miles, by a locomotive. The stone requires much labour to dress it. . . A ten-horse power engine is constantly employed for mixing mortar. About sixty masons and labourers are employed on this work; the number of workmen varies much, for though good wages are paid some of them generally leave after every pay day; sometimes as many as eight fresh hands are set on the works in a day. According to the opinion of the foreman it will be two years at the present rate of progress before the viaduct will be finished.

Opposite page: Etching of the partly-completed Smardale viaduct, in the Eden Valley. Notice the considerable amount of timber used as scaffolding.

Below: A Parliamentary Committee considering the Settle-Carlisle Bill. Notice the large map hanging on the wall. The Midland, having reached an understanding with its rival, the London and North Western, hoped to abandon the Bill in 1869 but was refused permission. When it was rejected, the Midland groaned and local landowners rejoiced; they could now appreciate the advantage of having a railway running over their land.

Above: John Allport, General Manager of the Midland Railway from 1860 until 1880. It was a stressful time. He was nicknamed "the Bismark of Railway Politics" by some of his contemporaries. When he was honoured by his friends in 1876, he said: "If I had one work in my life that gave me more anxiety than another, it was this Settle-Carlisle line."

BURIALS in the Parish of *Chapelle dale or Ingleton Fells*				
in the County of *York*			in the Year 18**74**	
Name.	Abode.	When buried.	Age.	By whom the Ceremony was performed.
Lewis Roberts No. 401.	Blea-moor in Ingleton Fells	July 19th	32	E. Smith. M.A Vicar
William Dyke No. 402.	Bleamoor Tunnel	Aug. 2nd	40	E Smith M.A Vicar
Sarah Grace Metcalfe No. 403.	Ingleton	Augt 31.	19 years	E Smith M.A Vicar
Sarah Ann Cameron No. 404.	Batty yeat	Sept. 15	1 year	E Smith M.A Vicar
Richard Wright No. 405.	Batty green	Nov 16th	25 years	T. Dod Sherlock Off. Min.
Robert Hepinstell No. 406.	The Tunnel Huts Ingleton Fells.	Nov. 17th	37 years	T. Dod Sherlock Off. Min.
James Smith. No. 407.	Chapel Le Dale.	Nov. 20th	21 years	T. Dod Sherlock Off. Min.

A PAGE FROM THE BURIAL REGISTER OF CHAPEL-LE-DALE CHURCH
IN 1874 WITH THE NAMES OF RAILWAY NAVVIES.

Ambulance and Bog Cart. The former was similar to one of the horse-drawn wagons being used during the opening up of the American West. The bog cart consisted of a barrel on a light chassis and was used for carrying materials in boggy country. The poor horse had to manage as best it could.

What was blasted out of tunnels or dug out of cuttings came in useful for the many embankments, such as one (pictured above) in the Eden Gorge where, after months of tipping, large sections might suddenly slip into the river. Notice how the artist has created a vast scale by drawing a diminutive train (near the skyline, right). In moving boulder clay, the railway-builders handled a material which was rock-hard in dry conditions and had the consistency of Yorkshire Pudding mixture when wet.

Embankment and Cutting

THE PULLMAN DAYTIME CAR OF THE TYPE USED WHEN THE SETTLE-CARLISLE WAS OPENED TO PASSENGER TRAFFIC. MANY VICTORIANS DID NOT CARE FOR IT BECAUSE IT LACKED PRIVACY.

The work hitherto has been attended with many impeding difficulties—such as the hardness of the stone, the flooding of the quarries by a mountain stream, and the wetness of the moor. The black marble, which is capable of a fine polish, is dug out in blocks. . . It is in mind to use additional mechanical forces so that double the number of workmen may be employed. A steam pump will be used at the quarry, and two steam travelling cranes on the gantry.

As the foundations of the piers and abutments are laid so deep, a cursory observer will not see the full extent of the progress made. Mr. Ashwell, the contractor, has done much to make the workmen comfortable. On the gantry, the men have boxes to shelter them from the weather and on the ground there are sheds for the comfort of the masons. The wages on these works average from 1s. to 1s. 6d. per day higher than the wages in Lancashire and Yorkshire; many of the masons get 6s. 6d. per day.

L.G. (1871)

The masons of Batty Moss Viaduct, Dent Head Viaduct and some other portions of the Settle and Carlisle. . . have been on strike for more than a week. For 9 hours per day they had 6s. 3d. and as the contractors required them during the summer months to work 10 hours per day, with the addition of 8d per extra hour, they have struck work. It is not reported whether there is any prospect of a speedy agreement between the men and their employers. For the sake of the completion of the new line, the sooner the dispute shall come to the end the better.

L.G. (1872)

It [Batty Moss Viaduct] will contain 30,000 cubic yards of masonry, besides 3,000 cubic yards of concrete, six feet of which is under nearly all the piers. The foundations were sunk 25ft in depth through peat, clay and washings before the solid rock could be met with, on which the viaduct stands...At the foot of the viaduct is a network of tramways, passing round the sharpest of curves, and up inclines as steep as 1 in 18, used for bringing stones, mortar, and other materials to the viaduct. There are also mortar mills, brick-making machines, drying sheds and kilns... We are shown the quarries for the Viaduct, which are formed by damming and altering the course of the river. The beds of rock are then taken out. Peat in this district seems to abound. Some we saw was 9 feet deep, but it is not used at all, coal being carted instead, as much as 600 tons a month being used on Contract No. 1.

W.A. (1873)

When leaving the viaduct, my guide hailed an engine driver who was about to return with a train of empty wagons to one of the cuttings in the direction of the tunnel; after mounting the engine and taking our position, so as to support ourselves by the brass rail on its side, the snorting steed started off at a tolerably quick speed.

No one can imagine the queer sensation which comes over one from the rolling and pitching motion of the locomotive caused by the unevenness and crookedness of the tramway excepting a novice in such a mode of transit. Up and down, heaving on one side and anon on the other, slackening its speed at curves and then accelerating it when they were past, was enough to make a nervous person giddy and to relax his hold.

It was a relief when the locomotive had accomplished its journey to alight safe and sound on terra firma.

L.G. (1871)

Engines are being fixed upon the southern and northern summits of Bleamoor, which is 1,753ft high. The heavy material is drawn up a steep tramway on the northern side of the moor by means of three "crabs" placed at different distances on the route, and platelayers' trollies. A similar tramway will shortly be laid on the south side of the moor when crabs will be superseded by the engines now in course of erection. Donkeys are employed on the south side for carrying coals and other light materials in sacks. The water and debris are now drawn from the shafts by horses, but shortly engines will be employed for that purpose at all the shafts except No. 4, which is on the north side of the moor.

L.G. (1870)

The cuttings on this (South) side of Blea Moor Tunnel are well opened up, the gullets being well driven in advance. About 150,000 cubic yards have been taken out. Two locomotives are employed in conveying the excavated earth to the bank and about 150 men are employed at these cuttings. The number of men fluctuates very much. At present there is ample room for double the number. Most of the work on this part of the line is let to Batty Moss gangs and the men divide their earnings equally among themselves, or in proportion to the hours they work. The men, on account of this co-operation, earn good wages and they might do well but for drink. Drink meets them at every step and they appear to be powerless to resist the British workman's greatest foe.

L.G. (1871)

At the south end of Blea Moor Tunnel all appeared to be life and activity. The chatter of machinery, the noise of children and men indicated that no ordinary work was going on. As we reached the south end of the tunnel a train of trollies was about to ascend the steep tramway to the summit of Blea Moor. This mountain line is worked by a wire rope and a fixed engine on the hill. Most of the trollies were laden with coal, which were crowned with bags of flour and other domestic commodities. Before an engine was erected, coals were carried up the mountain by donkeys, and heavy railway material was drawn up by "crabs".

L.G. (1871)

Shaft A, sunk at the proposed entrance to the south end of (Blea Moor) tunnel, is 35 yards deep. About 100 yards have been driven or tunnelled northwards. The lining of the arch with brickwork varies from 1ft 6 inch to 2ft 3inch in thickness completed. At this shaft, a 12-inch winding engine is employed, which also works an 8 inch pump and a Blow George to supply the men below with air.

No. 1 shaft is a permanent shaft which has been sunk to the foundation level. About 40 yards from this shaft have been tunnelled each way, and the arching of the top has been completed as at A shaft. A 12 inch winding engine is used to draw the debris from the tunnel. A 16 inch engine is employed to pump the water and blow air to the men at the bottom.

No. 2 shaft is also a permanent shaft and it has been sunk to foundation level, a depth of 127 yards, and lined throughout with brickwork so that operations will soon be in full force for taking out the tunnel and driving headings. A 16-inch winding-engine is used to draw up the debris from the tunnel and a 20 inch engine is fixed for working the pump, which is a 10 inch one, the same as No. 1. The water met with varies from 80 to 100 gallons per minute. Engine power is laid down to raise 450 to 500 gallons per minute.

The heading from the north on Dent Head end has been driven a distance of 750 lineal yards, or nearly half a mile, into the hill and is fast approaching the summit. It has been driven under No. 3 shaft, which has been standing for some time.

At this end, the air is supplied to the workmen at the face of the heading by a simple and effectual contrivance, viz. a long column of water in a wrought-iron pipe, which has its outlet through a rose fixed on the tip. The column of water has a pressure of 120lb per square inch. Consequently, the rush of water drives the air up a

Continued on page 73.

ARTIST'S IMPRESSION OF A MINER AT WORK IN BLEA MOOR TUNNEL.
DYNAMITE COST £200 A TON. THE BILL FOR CANDLES WAS £50 A MONTH.

Above: John Sydney Crossley, the Engineer-in-Chief for the Settle-Carlisle Railway, was the Midland's man on the ground. In 1865, he and Allport walked most of the way looking for the most practical course their new railway might take. The chief obstacle was a dome-shaped hill, Blea Moor. Crossley staked out the sections, concerned himself with the design of the viaducts and made monthly reports on progress to the Midland directors. He had delayed his retirement to see the line through to completion; he was so exhausted that he died in August, 1878.

Above: An artist's impression of Birkett Cutting, above Mallerstang. When Birkett Tunnel was driven, the engineers were impressed by the much varied strata of the fault-line. Apart from limestone and grit, the miners struck slate, iron, galena and even coal.

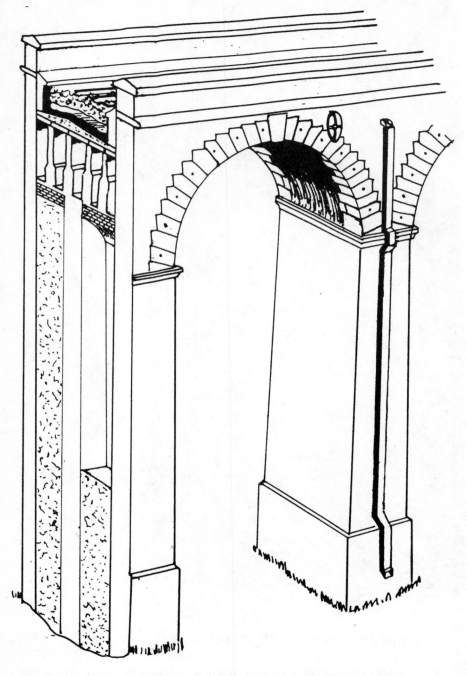

THIS SKETCH SHOWS THE ANATOMY OF ONE OF THE ARCHES OF
RIBBLEHEAD VIADUCT.

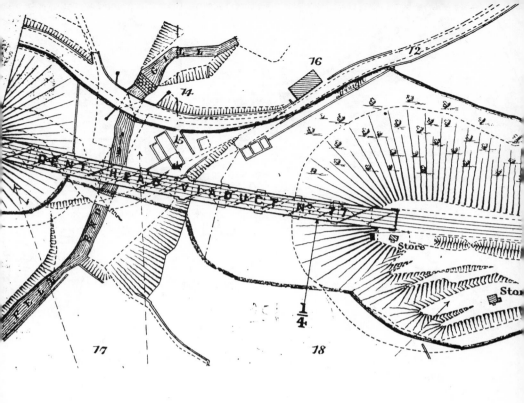

A survey of the Settle-Carlisle led to the compilation of a detailed plan showing not only the big structures, such as viaducts, but station facilities like cattle docks, lineside buildings of the platelayers and even the naptha stores, used to store the commodity which was then used to illuminate tunnels. Denthead Viaduct (above) is listed as Bridge No. 77 and spans Fell End Gill. Notice the hatched areas at either end, indicating the steep embankments.

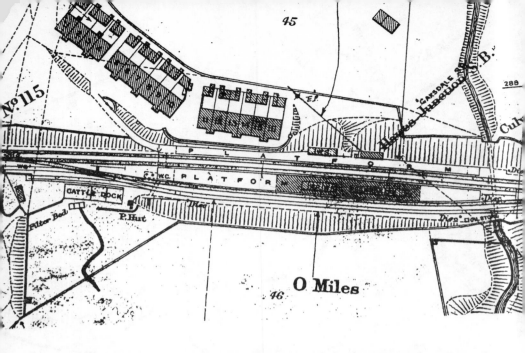

From the Land Plan we see the platform, buildings and railway servants' cottages at Garsdale.

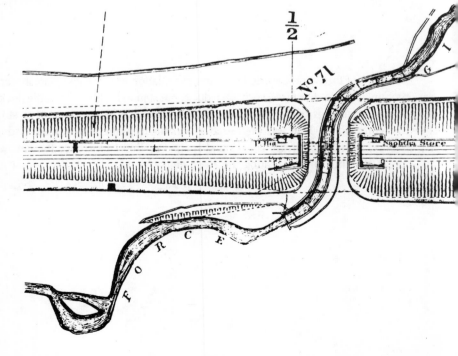

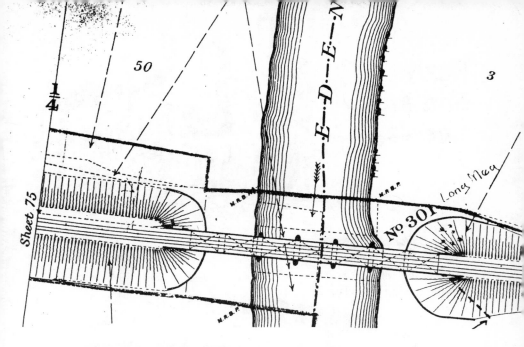

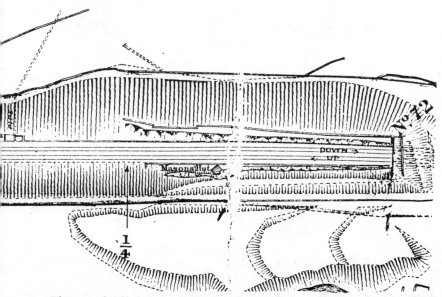

Details of Eden Lacy viaduct (also known as Long Meg), spanning the River Eden and numbered 301.

The stretch of line just south of Blea Moor Tunnel (No. 72). An aqueduct carries Force Gill Beck over the railway.

Early Midland Loco's

Top to Bottom: Kirtley 2-4-0, built in 1866. Kirtley 0-6-0 goods of the 1860s. A re-built version of Johnson's class 2P 4-4-0.

pipe 11 inch by 9 inch to the face of the heading. The force of the air is so strong it will blow a candle out two or three yards from the end of the pipe.

The whole of the tunnel, with very little exception, is hard rock, such as limestone and grit. The average speed of driving at a face is about four yards per week. Though there are about 160 miners at work in the tunnel, still there is sufficient room for twice that number.

L.G. (1871)

For about 350 yards the Tunnel is on a curve; it is then straight for the rest of the distance. At No. A Shaft, the level of the railway is 1,151ft above the sea, the incline for 11½ miles being nearly 1 in 100 for the whole distance.

There are seven stationary engines on the Tunnel, two for winding materials up the incline planes from each end, the rest for pumping and winding the excavations up and for lowering bricks and mortar down the shafts. The miners also use this means to get to and from the Tunnel. At the top of the Tunnel there is a self-acting incline. The loaded trucks coming down draw the empty ones up to a millstone grit quarry which is used for obtaining stone for concrete and sand. The absence of the latter material has greatly increased the expense of mortar.

W.A. (1873)

The Tunnel is in a great state of forwardness and in most places the arches are turned. Some of the side walls are of brick, while in other places the arches are turned on the solid rock. . . The tunnel for the greater proportion of its area is driven in solid rock, and the difficulties met with in some part of the operation arise from spontaneous combustion of the rock after the advanced headings have been driven. As this is a source of much danger to the workmen, great care is needed while carrying on mining and other operations. The works on many occasions have thus been retarded, and even now, though some of the faces are in the hardest rock, it is necessary to use timber to protect the workmen.

There are about 300 miners, bricklayers and labourers employed in the tunnel and the works are being pushed on with considerable force. The entrance to the south end of the tunnel is at present barred by a stout piece of cutting, which it is hoped will be taken out by August, when there will be a communication from one end of the tunnel to the other without descending any of the shafts. The strata met with in the tunnel is black limestone and gritstone, with a few beds of shale.

In the tunnel there are two bricklayers for each side, who have each one labourer, and there are two mortar carriers for the whole of the bricklayers. These bricklayers with their servers will lay about 35,000 bricks in three days. About 70,000 bricks are used in the tunnel weekly. Ten locomotives and 18 portable and stationary engines are in constant use on No 1 Contract and about 1,800 men are employed.

No person can walk in the tunnel for an hour or more and listen to the thundering reports and reverberations of blasting, see the miners wielding with terrible force their sledge-hammers when drilling the hard rock, and breathe the thick smoke of the exploded dynamite, without feeling sympathy for those employed in such mining operations, and of seeing what a privilege it is to travel by rail at the rate of a penny per mile.

L.G. (1873)

The temperature of the Headings before they were joined was 80 degrees; when the passage was through, the thermometer read 57, showing a difference of 23 degrees.

W.A. (1873)

The Headings have met correctly, within 3 inches we are told, a distance of 924 yards having been driven from the two ends. The strata is Limestone, Gritstone, Gritstone beds, and shale. In some parts the tunnel requires no lining; in others the roof only is lined and in places it is lined throughout. The lining is of brickwork and varies in thickness from 1 ft 6 inches to 3 ft...Black damp has been met with in the Heading, and also an explosive stone. It is supposed that there is compressed air in the hill which forces the stone outwards when partly excavated.

W.A. (1873)

In the Tunnel, the work never stops from Sunday night at ten, until Saturday night at the same time; relays of men relieving one another at 6 a.m. and 6 p.m. It is formed by hand drilling, filling the holes with gun-cotton or gunpowder, and then igniting by means of a time fuse. The debris is then cleared away, either up the shafts in "skeps" or in waggons at the open end; the brick lining follows as soon as possible. The light is obtained by means of tallow candles, and has a pretty effect. About 16 yards of tunnel are done in a week, although here and there we see water dripping and the engines pumping.

W.A. (1873)

After leaving Blea Moor tunnel at the north end, the Dent Valley opens to view and is crossed by a pretty Viaduct of 10 arches, the same span as the Batty Moss Viaduct, with one thick pier in the centre. The height is 100 feet above Fell End Gill. This Viaduct, the road bridge, with the farmhouse at its foot, and the road winding down by the side of the hill, form altogether a most picturesque scene. There are two large quarries on this side of the hill, for supplying this Viaduct with stone.

W.A. (1873)

Contract No. 2:
Dent Head to Kirkby Stephen

Arten Gill Viaduct is the first great work on Contract No. 2 and consists of 11 arches, the same size as those of Batty Moss Viaduct, but 120 feet high in the deepest part: by diverting the line the viaduct was made 50 feet less in height, as it now crosses over the top of a waterfall instead of the bottom.

W.A. (1873)

Artengill Viaduct is a work of considerable difficulty, and it has been carried on under many disadvantages. The works of late had been much retarded through the breaking of the machinery for lifting stone. The gill is very deep and rugged, and its sloping banks on each side are very steep. Before the viaduct was begun there was a waterfall of 60 foot descent, which is now partly filled up with debris.

The viaduct is 235 yards in length, and consists of ten piers and two block piers. The block piers at their base are 42ft by 28ft, and the smaller piers are 38ft by 15ft. The piers are 45ft apart, and the highest is 103ft to springing, and 26ft above that will be rail level. The foundations are all on rock, and some of them are 60ft below the surface.

L.G. (1872)

By diverting the line, the height of Artengill Viaduct was reduced more than 50 feet, as it crosses a waterfall at the top side instead of the bottom, as originally intended, and this without any decrease in the radii of the curves. It is built in blue limestone obtained from a quarry in the side of the hill close by; the same class of stone is cut and polished at Mr. Nixon's marble works in the valley and is used for mantel-pieces and such like articles...

W.A. (1874)

Great difficulty was met with in getting foundations for the piers. Some are more than 55 feet below the surface of the ground, the timbering and strutting to support the ground looking quite a mass of wood in all directions. At a short distance from the Viaduct is an occupation bridge which was also the cause of much expense in the foundations, for after sinking 30 feet deep, piles were obliged to be driven another 25 deeper into the ground.

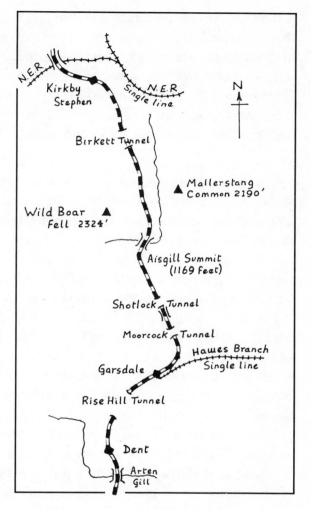

W.A. (1874)

Between Artengill Viaduct and Rise Hill or Black Moss tunnel, there are some very heavy works. An occupation bridge to the high moors, though as a rule a matter of little difficulty, in this case proved, on account of the nature of the soil, a serious undertaking. After sinking the foundations 30ft it was found necessary to rear the superstructure on piles driven 25ft deeper. A little futher on the line there is a deep cutting containing 95,000 cubic yards.

L.G. (1873)

Kell Beck culvert was, owing to the state of the ground, built in steps, and as there are from 20 to 30 breaks in the descending underground watercourse, the repeating falls of the mountain stream have a pleasant effect on both the eye and the ear. On the east side of this culvert a number of men were employed getting stone from an immense quarry, out of which rocks had been dug for most of the bridges and culverts in the neighbourhood.

The next cutting is one of considerable length and depth, containing 150,000 cubic yards, and over which the coal road from Lea Yeat runs by Helmsike Hill and Alick's Fold to the coal pits, which are at an elevation of more than 1,700ft above sea level. Shortly beyond this cutting there is a very large embankment over Cowgill containing 160,000 cubic yards of filling.

At the bottom of the gill is the largest culvert on the contract, measuring 540ft in length, and the opening for the stream, which is a pointed or Gothic arch 16ft by 10ft in width. The mason work of this culvert is of great strength, rendered necessary by the superincumbent matter and the immense quantity of water which will flow through it in heavy rains. The height of the embankment in the centre of the stream is 80ft, and at the south west of it about 100ft. Workmen were building on this side of it an immense dry breast-wall, 50ft high, to prevent the embankment from slipping away.

L.G. (1873)

Cow Gill [south of Dent] is crossed by an embankment about 100ft in height. The culvert is a gothic arch in shape and 540ft in length. The embankment has to be dry-packed with stones for 50ft in height to prevent it slipping away. In this Gill stones full of iron pyrites were discovered.

W.A. (1874)

It is supposed that a station will be made near the Cowgill coal road. At one time it was in contemplation to make it at Dent Head. Whichever site may be fixed upon, the ascent to it will be steep and difficult.

L.G. (1875)

At the bottom of Rise hill or Blackmoss we came to a deep and wide gully, through which runs Cowgill beck. Many disasters of a nature to retard operations have occurred during the progress of the work on account of the frequent rains and floods. At times it was impossible to go on. As it was impracticable to divert the stream in consequence of the gully on both sides being so steep, the staging and other materials were frequently washed away.

The filling up of this gully will be a great and a difficult operation on account of its great depth, and the miry nature of the earth in the immediate district. Although it was calculated that it would take about 200,000 cubic yards of earth to fill up this gully, now it is thought that it will take 155,000 cubic yards more.

At these works there are a mortar mill and two powerful steam cranes. The stone, as at Artengill Viaduct, is laid in Crossley cement.

L.G. (1872)

There are now about 1,400 men employed on No. 2 contract, and since the works were begun about 17,000 men have "jacked up" as it is called. It is true that some of the 17,000 were discharged from the works, but the great bulk left of their own accord.

L.G. (1872)

79

A deal of plant in this locality (above Dentdale), which was conveyed from Kirkby Stephen on to the line at a great cost, has not only been useless for want of workmen, but has fallen to decay. Indeed, there is such a lack of men, that four could be employed where there is only one.

L.G. (1872)

Being curious to see what was going on in Black Moss (Rise Hill) tunnel, I descended with two of the men into number one shaft. The gloom in the rocky excavation, the hammering of drills, the voices of the men and the dim lights of candles gave to the murky scene a novelty that will long be remembered...Some idea may be formed of the hardness of the rock when it is stated that thirty-five drills have been blunted with 18 inch boring. The atmosphere is so close in the tunnel that the men have to strip to their flannels. In blasting the rock it requires more than ordinary care as sometimes pieces of 15cwt fly to the distance of 20 yards.

L.G. (1872)

The cutting at the entrance of [Rise Hill] tunnel is attended with numerous difficulties; consequently the progress is very slow. The side of the hill is breaking away in many places, and the excavated matter is little else but what is called in railway parlance "slurry" or slush. One of our informants remarked that it was nothing but slurry and boulders and that the slurry stuck to the tools like treacle. Some of the water-marked boulders are three tons in weight. The slurry is chiefly removed by grafting tools and water buckets.

L.G. (1872)

At No. 2 shaft [Rise Hill tunnel] there are a blacksmith shop, eight huts, miners' cabin, store-room and engine-house. The engine is a double cylinder one, of twenty horse power, and used for blowing air into the tunnel and lifting the debris from the excavation. At No. 2 shaft there are a steam engine of twenty-five horse power, and a double cylinder of twelve horse power, for drawing up the steep ascent from Garsdale coals, provisions and railway material. There are also a blacksmith shop, a general store-house, a mortar mill and five huts...From the summit of Rise Hill, we descended the steep incline at a quick rate in bogies. It was a trial of a man's nerves who was not accustomed to such a mode of locomotion. At the bottom of the hill were numerous huts, a weighing machine, stabling for ten horses and a blacksmith shop.

L.G. (1872)

Black Moss or Rise Hill tunnel, one of the heaviest on the line, is mined from two shafts 170ft deep, and at the headings of the south and north entrances. The excavation is through solid and hard rock, some of the pieces weighing more like iron than stone. The tunnel is 1,230 yards in length and 26ft in width and 20ft in height. In the middle of it about 500 yards had been mined, in addition to a large heading of 250 yards, which had been driven beyond this point. About 120 miners are employed in the tunnel. Descending No. 2 shaft in an iron skip one was soon down at rail level, when the mining south and north was examined, until one felt an ardent longing to see the brighter world above.

To a stranger there is something unearthly in the sounds and appearances of mining operations so far beneath the surface of the earth. Dimly burning candles, uncouth looking wagons standing on the rails or moving to and fro, men at the facings, some above and some below, with their numerous lights like twinkling stars in a hazy night, the noise of the twirling drills beneath the terrible force of big hammers wielded by stalwart men, and the hac-hac or half sepulchral groan at each stroke, the murky vapour, the chilling damp, and the thick breathing make a novice to such scenes feel a thrill of more than ordinary pleasure when he ascends to breathe the unpolluted mountain air.

It will be necessary to arch the tunnel with masonry, as the rock is so full of backs and joints it is not possible to mine the roof to the shape required. In some places, large pieces of rock have fallen and left the roof for 20 yards quite flat.

L.G. (1873)

Between the north end of [Rise Hill] tunnel and the junction with the Hawes line there is a long culvert in Cotes gill where the water on the Garsdale side falls 30 feet. The bank over this gill, on the low side especially, was made with difficulty, and it was necessary to buttress it with a stone wall containing 6,000 tons of stone. As the gill on both sides of the line is lined with trees, it gives an ornamental appearance to this portion of the moorland route.

L.G. (1873)

As an indication of the inaccessibility of this spot [head of Garsdale], we may mention that every tip wagon here used by the contractor had to be brought by road up from Sedbergh and that the carriage of them cost a guinea each.

M.R. (1876)

With Dandry Mire Moss embankment, which is near Moorcock, the miry state of the ground has given the contractors and managers an inconceivable amount of trouble and labour. Tipping went on for more than two years, and instead of a solid embankment being formed, the peat yielded to the weight of the filling to such an extent that it rose on each side of the line in the form of a high bank—in some places 15ft.

Finding after more than 250,000 cubic yards had been tipped that the bog would not sustain the weight of the clay and stone used for filling up, it was decided to make a viaduct in the deepest part of the moss—a viaduct of six arches, each of 45ft span. The greatest depth is 53ft, and for nearly the whole length it will average from 45ft to 50ft from foundation to top of the peat. The peat varies from 5ft to 15ft, the greater portion of which had to be dug out before the embankment which is to join the viaduct could be formed.

L.G. (1873)

Messrs. Benton and Woodiwiss, the contractors for making the line from Dent Head to Kirkby Stephen, requiring the services of a locomotive engine for earth work, received one by rail at Sedbergh on Monday last, named the *Lorne,* which was conveyed to Garsdale Head by about 20 horses. One or two slight mishaps occurred on the road owing to the great weight of the engine, but by the patience and perseverance of the men in charge they were overcome without much difficulty.

C.W.A. (1873)

Near the moss is the Moorcock bridge which skews at an angle of 70 degrees. This fine and massive-looking bridge which crosses the Hawes and Sedbergh road contains about 3,000 cubic yards of masonry. The structure, which is finished, with the exception of the coping stones, has a span of 35ft and it is 36ft in height. At the foot of the bridge on the Moorcock side is the boundary stone which divides the North and West Ridings.

L.G. (1872)

There are a few dreary cuttings before the summit of the railway is met with at Ais Gill Moor. The level of rails at the summit is 1,167ft above the sea. Near this spot, three rivers take their rise, the Eden, the Ure and the Swale. The railway follows the first-mentioned to Carlisle.

W.A. (1874)

Good progress is being made at Aisgill Viaduct, which consists of 4 arches 66ft high and 45ft span. The breadth of the piers at the base is 33ft, which taper to 29ft at the top. The length of the viaduct is 99 yards. The gill on the south side is very romantic and on account of its overhanging rocks it presents to the eye a very bold appearance. The stone which is dug from the gill on the high side is lifted to the viaduct by a steam jib crane.

L.G. (1872)

No. 19 bank down Mallerstang is 20 chains in length and 80ft in depth. The workmen on this bank have been tipping on the same metals for 12 months without getting the bank any higher on the top. The material is of such a loose and soft nature and made more slushy by the constant rains, so that instead of forming a permanent way, it spreads itself out in the valley.

L.G. (1872)

After passing through a heavy cutting [in Mallerstang], the line is carried along the Intake Bank, about 100 feet high. At this point an extraordinary circumstance occurred; the tipping proceeded for twelve months without the embankment advancing a yard. The tip rails, during the whole period, were unmoved, while the masses of slurry. . . rolled over one another in mighty convulsions, persisting in going anywhere and everywhere, except where they were wanted.

M.R. (1876)

Birkett Tunnel, the Burleigh Rock Drill is being used with good effect. This drill makes a hole a foot deep in five minutes, the same depth taking two men at least 40 minutes.

W.A. (1874)

At the south end of the Birkett Tunnel in the cutting, a very fine vein of lead ore has been cut and a Company are now driving levels underneath the Railway to work it out.

W.A. (1876)

Intake Embankment which for two or three years caused so much trouble and extra labour, on account of the slushy character of much of its tippings, is now an unyielding bank, equal to any on the line.

L.G. (1875)

In passing through Kirkby Stephen railway yard, we noticed the hospital for accidents, stabling for 25 horses, saddlers, blacksmiths, and carpenters' shops, and an engine for sawing wood, cutting hay and crushing beams and oats for 100 horses.

L.G. (1872)

A machine for excavating the boulder clay lies near here [Kirkby Stephen Station]. The machine is patented by two gentlemen engaged on the railway, but we hear diversity of opinion exists as to its capabilities. Being a trial machine many improvements are already seen in it, but the "modus operandi" is entirely new in construction and ingenious in design.

W.A. (1874)

Kirkby Stephen Station was in an advanced state and shortly it will be finished. A four-wagon goods shed was being roofed in. Six cottages and the station-master's house were finished. The station, which is a smart building, is built of freestone from Bradford and dressings from Barnard Castle. A good many men were employed in making cattle docks and by-sidings.

L.G. (1875)

The staging [at Smardale Viaduct] is up and many of the piers are being raised. One of the arches will span the South Durham line at an elevation of 38ft. The view down the deep and wooded glen with Scandal beck winding its course between the rugged banks, will have charms for sight-seers both in summer and winter.

L.G. (1872)

Smardale Viaduct consists of 12 arches, 45ft span, and will be 130ft high above the stream to rail level. It is built in grey limestone of most excellent quality from off the South Durham and Lancashire Union (North Eastern) Railway, about half a mile further up Scandal Beck. A complete absence of sand also in this Contract has added a large item to the expense, burnt clay being used instead of it, by permission of the Engineer-in-Chief, and it has been a most complete success.

W.A. (1874)

On Tuesday, the completion of Smardale Viaduct was celebrated by an interesting ceremony. The "last stone", on which was inscribed the following words—"This last stone was laid by Agnes Crossley, 8th June, 1875"—was well and truly laid by the lady.

Contract No. 3:
Smardale to Crowdundle

The Third Contract ends a little on the south side of Crowdundle beck, which divides Westmorland and Cumberland. The Company's resident engineer is Mr. Drage; contractor's engineer, Mr. Phillips; contractor, Mr. Firbank; manager, Mr. Throssel. On the Contract there are four locomotive engines, 17 portable engines and steam cranes, 1,400 men, 111 horses, 500 earth wagons, 2,000 tons of contractor's temporary rails in use, and several miles of permanent way laid.

L.G. (1873)

Crosby Garrett Tunnel is through solid rock, which is a mixture of limestone and grit, and at the heading, which was within 20 yards of the south entrance, the rock is mixed with flint, and is so hard that it is very difficult to excavate. The tunnel is 176 yards in length, and from the nature of the rock it will be necessary to line it throughout with brick. Nearly one hundred men are employed at this undertaking.

L.G. (1873)

At a short distance from Crow Hill, the Helm Tunnel begins, which is nearly 600 yards in length, 26ft wide and over 20ft in height. The sides are stone finished, and the arches are turned with brick. The entrances to the tunnel are faced with excellent freestone from a quarry in the neighbourhood. Though the interior of the tunnel has been finished some time ago, the last stones of the facing of the north arch were put in place on the

19th of June, before breakfast. At the Helm, not far from the tunnel there is an extensive hut village where brickmaking and various kinds of employment connected with the railway are carried on.

L.G. (1873)

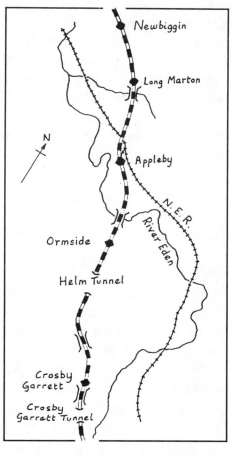

Ormside Viaduct, which is the first over the Eden, consists of nine piers and two block piers, and ten arches. The piers are of freestone and the arches will be turned with brick. From the bed of the river to the top of the parapet will be 100ft. The viaduct is at a short distance above the Clint rock, which stands out very prominently on the north side of the Eden.

L.G. (1873)

At Long Marton, one of the largest villages in the county, and at a distance of three miles north east of Appleby, there is a neat viaduct over Troutbeck. It consists of four piers and two block piers with five arches of 45 feet span. The height to rail level is 60ft. The arches are turned with brick and faced with red and white sandstone alternately. The quoins are red sandstone. This viaduct was all finished except one parapet.

L.G. (1873)

On Boxing Day, the mechanics and other officials in various departments engaged under Mr. Joseph Firbank, the contract for the Appleby section No. 3 of the Settle and Carlisle Railway Extension, met according to their annual custom—in whatever part of the world they may be engaged—to celebrate Boxing Day by a public dinner and entertainment. It took place at the *Crown and Cushion Hotel.* An excellent and substantial repast was prepared by the hostess, Mrs. Longrigg, to which between 40 and 50 did full justice to the good things provided. Mr. Brown Firbank occupied the chair. A number of toasts were interspersed with songs, recitations, etc. An agreeable and pleasant concert was accompanied by violin, concertina and banjo.

C.W.A. (1872)

On February 13, the ceremony of fixing the last brick in Helm Tunnel was performed by Mr. W.S. Fulton, of the Cumberland Union Bank, Appleby, in the presence of a large number of officials. The tunnel, which is about 600 yards long, was brilliantly lighted up for the occasion. A stage being erected in the centre, round which the company assembled, Mr. Fulton proceeded with trowel in hand to the top, and, having duly fixed the brick in the aperture, amid ringing cheers, intimated the successful completion of "The Helm Tunnel". He proposed in succession three cheers for Mr. Firbank, the contractor, Mr. Throssle, the representative of Mr. Firbank, and other officials connected with the works. Mr. Drage, the Company's engineer, said it was nearly two years since the first stone was laid in Helm Tunnel, which had been completed without loss of life or any serious accident.

L.G. (1873)

Contract No. 4: Crowdundle to Durranhill

On the line there are over 1,000 men, 70 horses, 4 locomotives, and 12 station engines. Mr. Allis is contractor, Mr. Lambert is head manager over the contract, Mr. Williams is manager and engineer of the south end of the contract, Mr. Stewart is resident engineer.

L.G. (1873)

In the deeply-wooded gill at Crowdundle Beck, about a quarter of a mile from Temple Sowerby. . . all was life and work and noise. The rattling of steam cranes, the puffing of engines, the clang of masons' and carpenters' tools, and the din of tongues and the singing of birds, were like life from the dead. . . The viaduct over the gill consists of three piers and two abutments, and four arches of 45ft span. The arches will be turned with red sandstone. To the coping stones from the surface is about 50ft. Some of the stones which were dug from Crowdundle quarry were of massive size.

L.G. (1873)

At Culgaith. . . there is a tunnel through a high bank in a forward state towards completion. It is 800 yards in length, 700 yards of which are completed. . . the sides and arches are of brick. The facings at the entrances of the tunnel are of blue Staffordshire brick, with string courses and coping of freestone. The excavation was through hard red marl.

L.G. (1873)

All the foundations at Eden Lacy Viaduct are in, and some of the piers are at springing, and the remainder are within 15 feet of springing. About a quarter of a mile from this viaduct a three arched ornamental bridge spans the line as an occupation way for Col. Sanderson of Eden Lacy House to pass from one part of his park to the other. This bridge is the finest piece of masonry on the Settle and Carlisle line, and its workmanship is a credit to both architect and workmen. The piers and arches are faced with rustic quoins, and the spring courses, parapets, and coping are all tooled and diamond hammered on the outward surfaces. The bridge, which was nearly finished, is built of old red sandstone, which with the superior workmanship gave it a unique appearance.

L.G. (1873)

At Eden Lacy viaduct, some difficulty was experienced by the engineers in getting a foundation down on the red sandstone, in consequence of the gravel that had accumulated in the bed of the river; and it became necessary to make a coffer dam. Accordingly, a double row of piles was driven into the bed of the river so as to form an oval; "puddling" was put between the two series of piles, to keep the water from running in; the water inside the oval was then pumped out by engines, and the foundation excavated and cleared.

M.R. (1876)

Shortly before entering Baronwood there is a heavy cutting through red sandstone, 660 yards in length and 50ft in depth. Some splendid blocks of stone had been dug from this cutting and used for many of the bridges and viaducts on the line. Though the cutting was finished, still on account of the excellent character of the rock a number of men were quarrying stone from the east side of the line for railway purposes.

L.G. (1873)

The Barren Park Cutting through red sandstone is a very heavy undertaking, as it is 42ft in its deepest place and nearly a mile in length. Just on the north side of Samson's Cave the line is cut out of the edge of a high bank, so that the west side of it has the appearance of a deep cutting while that on the east has the appearance of an embankment sloping down to the brink of Eden.

L.G. (1873)

After passing [southwards from Carlisle] under Duncowfold Bridge, a large tract of ground has been taken for ballast. The railway from this point to Armathwaite, along the rugged banks of the Eden, must have been very heavy work. After half a mile of filling there is a gorge over which the scaffolding is being erected in order to throw a small viaduct of three arches, in height sixty feet from the bed of the brook. Crossing this deep defile with some difficulty, three quarters of a mile brings us to what is known by the name of the slip at Eden Brows, and which the gangers say has been the heaviest part of this expensive line.

The railway rises here 120 feet above the bed of the river, and this deep gorge had to be filled in with earth. After many months' tipping it was found that the foundations were slipping—that is the

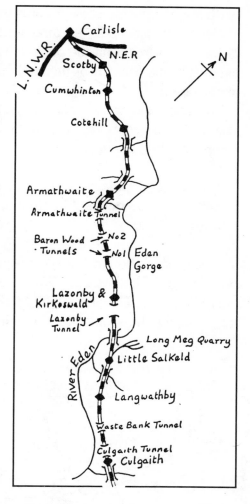

earth was moving en masse towards the river. Growing plantations shifted their position in this direction, and trees may now be seen growing 40 yards from the place in which they stood a few years ago, while the breadth of the river has been reduced apparently about one half.

Two years ago at this spot the men were tipping earth—to the number of 15 or 20. They are still tipping and the work is not yet complete, although very nearly so.

C.J.

At Carlisle a large area of land, perhaps 50 acres, is being prepared for the building of station, offices, goods warehouses, station yard., etc.

L.G. (1873)

The goods station at Carlisle covers 80 acres of land and comprises Engine Sheds, Goods Warehouses, Cattle Docks, Marshalling Sidings, etc. The present joint Carlisle passenger station is being enlarged and remodelled to admit of the new traffic.

W.A. (1876)

No. 6411 with the District Engineer's saloon.

Contract No. 5
(the Hawes branch)

This branch line is 5¾ miles in length and will be a single line... Mr. Story is the resident engineer and Mr. Crossley the head engineer... The cutting at the junction is finished, and for two miles from the terminus at Hawes the line is railed off. Two cuttings on the Hawes side are finished and three more cuttings are commenced. A road approach from Hawes to Moorcock and two occupation bridges and several culverts are finished, and a girder bridge is nearly finished.

Hawes Junction with the Midland is at Garsdale Head, where considerable works are to be erected. The platform walls were in progress and a number of cottages were being built. The works, when completed, will form a small village. There will be over twenty houses and an engine shed, besides a number of sidings for the exchange of traffic. It is reported that a large reservoir will be made to supply the engines and other places with water.

L.G. (1875)

A smallpox hospital has been built at Appersett for the men working in the North Riding district.

L.G. (1872)

PART THREE

The Footplate Men

WHAT THE navvies and engineers made, a dedicated railway staff maintained. My godfather, Ted Boak, was a driver on the Settle-Carlisle. He told of thrashing steam engines between Settle and the summit at Aisgill and of approaching Ribblehead viaduct in a gale, when he and the fireman—having seen that the firebox was glowing satisfactorily—crouched in sheltered corners of the cab and let the locomotive take care of itself as the wind howled about them. It's no wonder that every small boy wanted to be an engine driver...

A Driver's Life

FIRE, boiling water, steam—this is the process at work in a locomotive. Steam rises to work the valves, which are connected through rods and big-ends to the wheels. Basically, coal is burnt in a firebox. The fire gives off gases which pass through tubes surrounded by water. The heated water becomes steam, which rises to the top of the locomotive and to the regulator valve, under its distinctive dome. Injectors transfer water from the tender to the boiler and there are gauge glasses to enable the footplate men to check on the amount of water in reserve.

A driver who had a reputation for speed on the rails never did more than 30 miles an hour when driving his car. "I couldn't go fast enough on an engine." Another driver—"a gentleman through and through"—was an exceedingly fine engineman. "When he'd set the regulator, you would have an easy trip on any job. He would never alter that regulator. He would hardly ever sit down. His overalls were spotlessly clean, with a crease down them. He used to enjoy visiting Carlisle for the dialect. He would sit there and quietly mention the place of origin of any man who was talking. 'That chap's from Glasgow,' he would say. You got all the Scottish dialects in the Barracks at Carlisle. His brother, who was also on the railway, was quite different. He didn't keep himself tidy and he was usually as black as the ace of spades!"

A good driver was considerate to his fireman. When Jimmy Fishwick became a driver, he was told by a man he greatly respected: "Now, Jim, when you get driving, remember that if you are going to pass Lazonby in the time that's in the time book,

19 minutes, you will be knocking it out of your fireman. I always lose about five minutes to Low House. Now the Midland (Carlisle) men don't; they want to pass Low House in 13 minutes."

On a steam locomotive, the men used a special railway language. "To stop, nobody ever said 'stop'—a driver or fireman would shout 'whoa'. That was the word that everybody would re-act to. Shout whooooa—and bang goes the brake!"

The Black Five was considered "a good engine". It was a dual purpose engine, good for passenger or freight work. "It would take 53 wagons to Carlisle." A Hellifield driver, thinking about the Black Fives, recalled with special pleasure a 6B engine. "You got on a 6B engine and you never had any problems at all."

A driver had 15 bogies (456 tons) on his train one day. He should have had only 390 tons. "The so-called pilot from Kingmoor was riding in the train with the passengers. I was pressing on, keeping my own timings, and he frightened half the passengers to death by telling them I was going too fast. When I was relieved at Hellifield, the stationmaster said I was in trouble. 'The passengers are complaining that you were going too fast.' I met the pilot in the mess-room and told him off quietly. 'I said I would have been better without him'."

The fireman had to keep his eye on the signals, for the driver was not expected to cross the cab to look for them. Yet when he passed his examination as a driver, he was told never to accept the fireman's word that a signal was clear. "Signals were never placed as they are these days so that they can be seen easily. An old semaphore signal could be in somebody's backyard, high up on a post or round the corner! And, boy, when you were working on Carlisle 'road', you were looking all over the place... Coming from Carlisle you were always pleased to see the Star of Bethlehem, that 'distant' signal for Aisgill. As soon as you spotted that, you knew the hard climbing was nearly over..."

I asked a grizzle-grey driver: "Have you ever been stuck for steam?"

Laughter. "I've stuck for steam more times than thou has hair on thi 'eeard. Some fellers are numbskulls. Best time was when I had twelve month with a driver who'd been in t'first world war. When he came back, he was put in t'front of all them that had been made drivers while he had been away. We took days about. He fired one day, I fired the next. The way he worked, I worked. We never stuck once.

"But I've been stuck at every signal between South Junction and Delaney's and Aisgill. We only just clanked ower at Low House. And with between 60 and 80 pounds, neither of the injectors worked."

Hughes/Fowler 2-6-0- "Crab", No. 2770.

The loose-coupled goods train is now but a faint memory. Nearly every goods train on the Drag was loose-coupled. It called for a lot of experience and skill to keep the couplings tight. A driver benefited from the guard's knowledge of the "road". The guard applied the hand-brake of his van when going downhill. "It was said that some guards had a match box. They put some marbles in and they had it on the seat beside them. When the marbles moved to the far end of the box, the train was going downhill. If they came towards him, the train was going uphill! He then put his brake on or off, whichever way he wanted." In the days of loose-coupled trains, it was possible to see the wheels of a guard's van when the train was on a steep downward gradient; they were sparkling like Catherine wheels in the darkness as the guard kept the handbrake on to ensure the couplings were tight.

Some drivers did not like certain guards. "They were either reading a book or nodding off. . . You could brake the engine and put a shake on. That gave the guard a bit of a reminder to keep his mind on his job!" The driver of a passenger train with an attendant dining car was blamed for any breakages, whether or not he had an abrupt action while driving.

Bonnyface, the Bradford-Hawes express, was popular with drivers, one of whom recalls walking up the market town and buying a baby Wensleydale cheese at the Creamery for 3s. 9d. "I used to bring a cheese home in late autumn and we kept it in the pantry until Christmas."

I met a retired driver who pointed to one of his eyes and said: "I've a piece o' coal in. It'll be in when I dee. I might leave it to one o' them." He pointed to his family. They were not amused.

Shovelling to Carlisle

"WHAT was it like being a fireman up the Drag?" I asked a veteran.

"What was it like? Very enjoyable." He laughed immoderately.

"How much coal did you use?"

"How would I know? Some firemen were good; some were 'very light'. Some of them knew how to use the machinery; others didn't even even know if it were raining or not. They'd have been grossly overpaid if they were paid with holes out of washers. I can't put it no plainer than that. . . If the fireman was a rough feller, he could use owt up to four ton between Skipton and Carlisle. A feller what were sensible wouldn't reach three ton."

The fireman continued: "Also—and don't forget this—I for one used to give a hell of a lot of coal away. I never brok owt up what wouldn't go in t'hole. If it were too big to go in t'hole, it went over t'side. Platelayers or anyone else who cared about it could have it. There was a garden near t'railway. I used to pop big pieces into a bloke's garden, in among his bushes. He didn't mind as long as they were not near his greenhouse. When I retired, I bet he missed me aw reight."

I also heard of the old lady with a lineside garden who placed a row of empty bottles on the wall. No self-respecting fireman could resist throwing cobs of coal at the bottles. The old lady was assured of having plenty of fuel.

Every type of steam engine was fired in a different manner. The fire had to be built according to the shape of the firebox. "A good fireman sat with his eyes glued on the chimney top. There should be just a haze; if there was black smoke, the fire was not burning properly. As soon as the haze cleared, the fire was ready for some more coal. If you did not put some on within minutes, then the steam pressure came down. As the fire became dirtier, the fireman worked harder. He kept his eye on the chimney top. If the blast was constant, he 'fired' regular away. Seven shovelfuls. Three down either side. One under the door.

"If it was a freight train, with lumps and a lot of dust, you rested the blade of the shovel on the firebox mouthpiece and the blast would take it. If you had a lot of slack, you kept the bottom door up, the top flat open and you dribbled coal in. You let it take it where it wanted. That also mucked your tubes up."

The "firing shovel" was a long-bladed shovel, rounded at the back so that coal wouldn't slip off. An even more impressive shovel—the "clinker shovel" or paddle—had a shaft from five to six feet long. This shovel was used for cleaning the ashes from the firebox. "Before they allowed you to take the bars up, and push the clinkers and the fire into the ash pan, you had to use a 'paddle'."

A fireman at a time when Class 3s (0-6-0) were stabled at Hellifield recalled the extra protection from the weather. He had worked on the L and Y Railway, when "there was just something over top of your head, so to speak. . . The seat was made of iron and you had to get yourself a bit of wood. . . With the Midland, you had good shelter and a proper box to sit on."

On the demanding Settle-Carlisle, a driver regarded any new fireman with suspicion, sometimes with resentment. A Leeds man, recalling his first trip, says: "The driver was boss on the footplate; it was important to get on with him. This one was a boozing pal of my dad's but it made no difference to his attitude towards me.

"I kept the engine going, with steam to spare, all the way up the Drag. The driver actually smiled. As we were crossing Denthead viaduct, with the driver leaning out of the cab to look for signals, the wind coming down the valley caught hold of me and but for a handle I grabbed, I would have been blown off the footplate. On the way back, the driver gave me an orange at Garsdale!"

Sometimes a driver would lend a hand with "firing". He'd say: "Come out o' t'rooad. Give us 'od." And he would put a few shovelfuls of coal on the fire. "The Compound firebox was eleven foot. You were throwing coal eleven foot through a narrow hole. If you missed a place on a steam engine, when it was working heavily, the steam (pressure) would come down almost immediately. You got no smoke and the fire would burn unevenly. 'Tha's missed some.' So you opened the door and started again till you got the right place. It really was a skilful job."

Not many firemen could claim to have worked between Leeds and Carlisle without "sticking". Sometimes, a steam train on the Drag ran out of steam. "In all the years I was on, this never happened on the Settle side, but coming back it happened twice. Let's face it, if it was pouring down and you were shovelling water into a firebox, you'd come to a standstill."

Carlisle Kingmoor, in the 1930s, when a Leeds man became a fireman on the Drag, was an extremely busy place. "You 'booked off' and went to your lodgings for the off-duty spell. You left your engine in the 'engine line'. It was moved in stages to the 'ash pit'. There were two rows, with as many as 20 or 30 engines, waiting to have their fires cleaned. Men were cleaning full-time. It was an hour's job to do one engine."

A visiting fireman recalls walking down to the Shed at Carlisle and discovering with surprise that some of the cleaners and "put-back firemen" were older than his dad. "The cleaning rate was 36s a week. If you were firing, you got 57s. When you got put-back, you were put-back in rate as well. I was firing. I was getting fireman's rate. I felt sorry for some of the others who'd slipped back."

A fireman had time to build up his fire when the train was at the southern approaches to the Settle-Carlisle. From Skipton, there is a gradual climb to Delaney's, and from Delaney's the way is a gentle incline through Gargrave and Bell Busk. At Hellifield, the steam can be cut off. "The train would coast down to Settle Junction."

In Steam Time, a fireman's eyes were upon the "distant" signal. "It could be seen from the fireman's side. If it was green, you said to the driver: 'It's all off.' And then you got stuck in. You'd be firing all the time. You gave it more regulator. How hard the fireman worked depended on the type of locomotive, and how big a load you had. If he was 'firing' a Jubilee, hauling an express, he was working. Because of the beat, a Jubilee put it up into the atmosphere quicker than you could put it into the firebox."

A fireman built up the fire before reaching Blea Moor tunnel; he did not want to have to replenish it as the locomotive ran through 2,629 yards of darkness. "If the wind was the wrong way—for you!—and you were slipping a lot, all the exhaust gases came back into the cab, with a choking effect for the crew."

After the hard work on the Drag, the summit of the line was reached at Aisgill. "Then the driver was telling me to have my sandwiches and tea because we could free-wheel down to Kirkby Stephen. By the time we got to Appleby, we would be starting into it again on Lazonby Bank... Sometimes we changed over at Appleby. That was hard going because you had climbed all the way up the Drag, you'd dropped down the other side and when you'd been relieved by the Carlisle men at Appleby, you had to climb all the way back!"

A southbound train more often than not had a following wind. "It could be a cold wind. I've fired engines wearing my heavy railway mac. The heat of the fire was fantastic. My overalls were being scorched at one side and ice was forming on the bucket eight feet away."

Rain washed the muck from the tender. "It was never the cobs of coal—just the muck. The slurry. I've known days so wet that t'driver had to help out; he opened and shut t'firebox door after every shovelful. We had to keep yon fire warm!"

The fireman was expected to operate the water-cranes but some drivers would take pity on their mates and would disembark to turn on the water; then the fireman did not have to clamber off the back of the tender. "We'd arrive at Settle. The driver would stop his engine in a precise place so that when the arm of the crane was swung it would be just right for getting water. The fireman used to scramble over the coals and put the 'water bag' in. We always called it a 'bag'. It was made of leather, I've seen us take on water at Blea Moor when the bag's been frozen so hard that the fireman had to kick it in the hole."

Woe betide the fireman if he did not shut off the water in good time. The alternative was to flood the tender, washing coal and muck down on to the footplate. In normal times, the ever-active firemen kept the footplate clean. "When I wasn't shovelling, I used to sweep up. I don't need to tell you where all the muck went!"

It was hoped to pick up water at Garsdale troughs. The driver, after watching for signs of their approach, would suddenly say: "Gerrit in." And the scoop was lowered. "You had your eye on the water gauge, which was in front of you. As soon as it showed about three-quarters full, you started pulling the scoop out. The drivers wanted to see it filled right up to the top. One would say: 'We could hev got some more in there.' If the tank overflowed, you were in lumber. The fireman couldn't win!"

Among the freight engines stabled at Skipton were "the old Derby 4s." Each had a small tank. "If you had a heavy load, you'd leave Skipton with a full tank and hope to get some more water at Settle, which should then take you to Blea Moor. After that, you thought of the troughs at Garsdale, the highest in the world. You could get some more water at Kirkby Stephen, Appleby and so on."

The water troughs near Garsdale were 'hitty-missy'. A driver who had never missed getting water here used the effective but potentially dangerous practice of pulling out the steam brake. "I can't explain exactly what happened but as you pulled it out, you would see the water in the gauge shoot up a bit. You did this till you got to the end of the trough. But you had to be careful. You could have broken loose."

In times of hard frost, men were sent up to Garsdale troughs to keep them free of ice. A heating system was in operation. The workers slept in the platelayers' cabin and took provisions. "Jimmy Antell and Bob Lund were on that job for weeks on end," I was told by a driver who came to know them well.

Collecting water at Garsdale involved split-second timing. "You had the scoop to wind down into the troughs. A concrete post with an oil lamp was supposed to be a marker at night. Being an oil lamp, the marker had usually gone out. So on a pitch-black night, you counted bridges. One. Two. At the third bridge, the scoop must go in.

"Sometimes, you had followed close behind another train and the trough was still filling up with water. Sometimes, it was frozen up and we had to make a water-stop at Appleby. And sometimes, you'd hardly any water left. The driver got a bit jittery in case we couldn't make Appleby in time."

Wise drivers lowered the water scoop a little in advance of the Garsdale troughs. "I'd give it one or two turns on the wheel and then I wasn't wasting any time. Then I'd put it right down, but as soon as I saw the water gauge in the cab begin to move, I'd ease it back about half a turn. Otherwise, I'd be getting to the end of a trough with the tank getting full. I'd have a job breaking a column of water."

It was possible to get too much water—with messy consequences. "Many a time you'd be getting a tank full before you got half way along a trough and then water was splashing all over the place. If it was on a passenger train, in warm weather, and some passengers had their windows lowered, they got wet. It was the guard's duty to walk down the train to advise them to shut the windows.

"I was very fortunate one day. I had a camera with me. I was after a shot down the valley but it was a hazy day. So I took a picture down the side of the locomotives as we got water at Garsdale. You could see the cylinder taps were spitting and one or two spots of water had come on to the window."

A Victorian print of a locomotive almost buried by a snowdrift.

Wind and Rain

THE ELEMENTS conspired to test the footplate men. Tinted leaves falling in autumn might inspire the poet but when they were wet they settled on the tracks on a shadowy stretch like Stainforth Cutting, bringing many a proud train to a standstill, though its wheels continued to spin. "You just had to get yourself out of a predicament like that the best way you could." The ultimate solution was to bring up another locomotive. "They put one behind you to push you up."

The most famous weather story of the Settle-Carlisle concerns the locomotive on the turntable at Garsdale. It was blown round and round, out of control, by a strong wind. Afterwards, a barrier of sleepers was raised round the turntable to cheat the wind. "Same sort o' thing happened to us one day but before it started to spin, my mate climbed on and shifted it an inch or two, putting it out o' balance. Yon engine stopped itself. We had to send for some assistance from t'station to help us finish pushing it round."

Ribblehead was also a weather station from which coded messages were telephoned hourly to the Air Ministry. A driver relates: "I got to Ribblehead one day and the Stationmaster asked me to put some more coal on the fire. 'I want to see which way the wind's blowing,' he said. 'He did that once or twice with me, over the years'."

A driver could tell as he arrived at Ribblehead station what the conditions were likely to be at the viaduct. "With a westerly gale, you got gusts coming right down between Ingleborough and Whernside. It was like somebody blowing down a funnel. I used to say to the fireman: 'Look out, I'm going to knock hell out of the engine.' I always kept going, though. Many a time I've looked back and seen wagon sheets being ripped off and just blown away in the wind like pieces of paper... Then you had to stop at Blea Moor. Men were fastening sheets down. Many a time, you got stopped when you wanted to keep going!"

Wagon sheets were large and heavy. "I've been near Ribblehead viaduct in wild weather when a sheet blew off a wagon. That sheet floated away on the wind like a piece of confetti. It was going uppards, not downwards. I kept thinking—if that lands on a passing car, the driver won't see daylight again for ages!"

Ribblehead Viaduct could be a nightmare in a westerly gale. "The old Class 4 loco. hadn't much cab. If the wind was strong, you got your fire prepared before you got on to the viaduct, and then you and your driver got tucked away in a corner and let the engine chuff across. Three motor cars were blown off a special train at the end of Blea Moor loop."

The severity of the weather at Ribblehead when the wind came from the west is illustrated by the story of the crew of a Derby 4 being worked to Carlisle; they had to "go inside" at Blea Moor. "The rain was torrential. The wind was so strong it was blowing rain into the cab. George and I walked round the framing in the pouring rain and then stood in front of the smoke box outside. We were drier outside the engine than we'd been in the cab!"

In frosty weather, the trackbed on Arten Gill viaduct used to lift. "It was like driving over a corrugated roof. By heck—you hadn't got to go so fast over it. There were always flagmen out when these conditions prevailed. You got stopped and told of the conditions."

In Blea Moor, during the wintry spell of 1963, were icicles as big as... [words failed him]. "They knocked all t'brass handles off t'coaches of t'Carlisle slow as it went through..."

In steam days, there were worse tunnels than Blea Moor. "One was Mossdale, between Garsdale and Hawes, because we used to have to go tender first. It wasn't a very deep tunnel-top. There used to be icicles, stalactites—call 'em what the heck tha likes—and as we were coming down they were breaking off at tender-end and dropping on t'footplate."

When dealing with drifts across the line, the driver of a locomotive with a snow plough was expected to open the regulator, increase speed and barge into them. "You had an engine leading and an engine trailing. They were back to back. Each was equipped with a plough, so you could plough one way and plough back again. You would have a brake van in the middle." If the plough did not clear the snow, another "charge" was planned. "Snow used to come up through the footboards and from t'sides; there were sheets to stop it coming from above, but they weren't always effective."

A locomotive inspector who rode with the crew when snow-ploughing was taking place attracted attention because he was so well dressed. "He was new to the district and turned up with a beautiful blue Melton overcoat, smart suit, a Homberg and rubber boots on his feet. Usually, an inspector wore his oldest clothes, with an old donkey jacket and wellingtons."

3F 0-6-0 Midland locomotive of the type which hauled Settle-Carlisle freight until mid-century.

That Terrible Moor

THE SHAFTS of Blea Moor were equipped with "garlands" as part of the drainage system; water from a garland found its way into a downpipe which was connected with the main drain of the tunnel. After heavy rain, the driver of a steam locomotive might still be soaked while passing under a shaft. He often had his head out of the cab, looking ahead. He tried to avoid doing this in the tunnel, "otherwise, you had a stream of water down the back of your neck!"

Leeds men were the butt of many a joke by the footplate men of Skipton and Hellifield. "There was a smart Leeds feller—I hope he hears about this or reads this; it will sarve him reight—who said: 'Nah then, you're working at the third ventilator in the tunnel. I'm going to ride with yer to make sure you don't overshoot it.'

"I said: 'You needn't bother, lad. I'll hit third ventilator spot on wi' t'tender end; will that do thi?' He said: 'You won't see it.' I said: 'You don't knaw it all, even if thou does come fra Leeds.' So anyway, we entered the 'ole. He insisted on riding on t'engine. He worn't watching me, but when we got to approaching the second hole my hands were out o' t'cab, feeling for t'watter dropping out of t'ventilator shaft.

"Then when we were half way between theer and t'next 'un, a feller passed us rolling it out [a passing train emitted a lot of smoke!] so there were nowt visible. I started going slow from thereon, of course. He said: 'We aren't there yet!' I said: 'I knaws; shut thee gob.' When I felt t'watter, I was almost on t'point o'stopping—stalling, they call it—and I stopped and said to 'im: 'If thou walks back a yard or two, thou'll find thissen half way under the ventilator.'

"After a quarter of an hour or so, he came back and said: 'Can you see in this murk?' I said: 'Yes.' He said: 'By gow—that's a wonderful asset.' See? I couldn't see through that murk: who could? Nobody!"

The signalman at Blea Moor box cut the hair of visiting railwaymen. "He got quite a bit of custom because crews waited in the box for the arrival of trains from Carlisle; they would change over with the Carlisle men. One evening, just after haytime, I was waiting in the box when I heard a clomping on the steps and into the box came six farmhands. They all had their hair long, like hillbillies. The signalman started cutting their hair and I swept it up to keep the box clean.

Some of the permanent way men and their families lived in cottages the railway company built at the lineside near Blea Moor signal box. It was a lonely spot. A platelayer's wife regarded it as a good day out when she had a trip on the express called *Bonnyface*. She was taken through to Hawes and was back home an hour or two later. "That woman left her home on one day in the week and at holidaytime." I was told.

A driver who took water and coal to Blea Moor on the Carlisle pick-up said: "The wagon of coal was put off by Blea Moor box and the platelayers shovelled it off."

Bill Davison, a member of the Tunnel Gang for nineteen years, was a Methodist local preacher who sometimes took a service at Dent. He carried his bike through Blea Moor tunnel, rode down the dale to Dent Town and returned by the same route. "It was quiet in Blea Moor Tunnel on a Sunday." said Bill.

Some Drivers' Yarns

TO HEAR one of the old drivers tell a tale about the line, using a smattering of dialect to emphasise some telling point, was to come close to experiencing the true spirit of those who manned the steam trains on the Settle-Carlisle railway.

A Skipton man was the driver of a No.3 goods engine, heading south from Carlisle on a hot day early in the 1939-45 war. He recalled for me how he stopped at Garsdale and picked up a man with a plausible story who then went to collect a most suspicious parcel.

"We were not doing bad for steam but we were overloaded, which we all were at that time. We had to stop for water at Appleby and Kirkby Stephen. I said to my fireman: 'We'll stop at Garsdale because passenger train (Bonnyface) will have gone from Hawes. My bottle's empty.' He said: 'Are we all right for stopping?' I said: 'Oh, aye—we're bound to be. T'passenger will have gone and it's got to clear Dent Head before they'll let us clear Garsdale. Take your time.'

"We stopped at the island platform. While we were filling our bottles and drinking, this fellow walked round and he had a brief case. He said: 'Fine day, chaps.' I said: 'Aye—and you're getting your share of it.' He said: I'm getting more than my share of it...where are you going to?' 'Skipton.' 'Is Skipton this side of Settle or the other side?' 'Other side. What for?' 'Because the only chance I have of getting a ride is to persuade YOU to take me.'

"I asked to see his ticket. He had a day's excursion ticket, Settle to Hawes return. I asked him why he'd missed the train. 'Well,' he said, 'I thought I had time to walk it from Hawes to Garsdale.' He had allowed himself an hour and three-quarters. I said: 'Well it worn't enough to start wi'. But secondly, thou's bin calling. . .' (at public houses) He said he'd had one or two calls.

"I said: 'Oh, well—can ta keep thi gob shut?' He said: 'what do you mean?' I said: 'Exactly what I said. If thou starts blowing it in a club or a pub or anywhere where there's somebody 'at matters, about having a ride on an engine between Garsdale and Settle, two fellows here 'I'll get t'sack.'

"He said he could keep it dark. So he got on t'engine. He shoved his brief case in. He then shoved our lodging basket to each side, then went back where he'd come from and returned wi' a roll o'sacking (a side of bacon).

"We set off. There was Horton pick-up in front of us—that was definite. It stopped at Stainforth and Settle and then it was a toss up if Bentham pick-up had gone or not. We had Hawes pick-up behind us. As we entered the hole (Rise Hill Tunnel), smoke were pouring out: it were one of them days. Me and my fireman had our eyes on 'im. Fireman said afterwards: 'His eyes came out like chapil hat-pegs when we hit this smoke-bank and went in. I thought he was going to jump off.'

"When we got out, t'other end, he were the colour of a corpse. Blea Moor were worse. And, of course, it's a bit longer. And he was at side where watter spattered in. Anyhow, we got out. We got stopped at Ribblehead. It was nobbut a check; not a real stop. At Stainforth, we got stopped proper. I said: 'We'll be here twenty minutes, owd lad. Thou's nearly time to walk it to Settle.'

"He asked how far it was. I said: 'I've never walked it; I couldn't tell you. I reckon it would take half an hour; but it might not take half an hour wi' that lot.' He said: 'How will I get off at Settle?' I said: 'There ain't no difficulty about that. I will stop. We'll put the water-bag in and when the road is clear I'll set you down on t'muck and I'll see you on the road. Then you'll have to find your own way. But keep your gob shut.'

"I nivver heard owt from that day to this—whether he telled somebody or whether he didn't—but I can imagine him swanking."

Here's a tale heard at Skipton:

"I was on at 5-19am. Well—that were t'train time! I've actually forgot t'loading. I think we'd about 19 o'them things that took iron ore. We were Carlisle next stop, of course. Now to cut a long story short—if I could pass Appleby before Thistle Plaster pick-up left Appleby, I could reach Carlisle in time to be lifted off that engine and go and catch from Durran Hill sidings the 10-15 Birmingham.

"I knew all them lads. They'd stop outside Shed at Skipton for me to drop off so that I wouldn't have so far to walk. One of t'reasons were that whenever I double-headed them to Aisgill, I always left them the water at Garsdale troughs. They'd come a bloody long way, hadn't they? In other words, I did my duty.

"I just had a guard. I won't mention his name. He's deeard, though. He worn't well-liked at Skipton. 'I said: 'Nah then—kick thee brake off!' He said: 'What for?' I said: 'Because I want 10-15 out o'Carlisle.' He said, slowly: 'You want to be careful today.' That's all. He didn't say t'war's ower nor nowt. I said: 'Thee keep thi brake off. I'll do t'rest.' I had to stop at Stainforth because he'd left a brake pinned down. Shows how I were shiftin'.

"Then away we went. We didn't get stopped till we got to Appleby. I did notice, subconsciously, that there were nothing on the up-road. We passed one of the Scots—only one—in Blea Moor Tunnil. The other, seemingly, had been cancelled—unbeknown to me. I went into t'Box at Appleby, to see what we were stopping for and to try and get to knaw whether Thistle Plaster had gone.

"The only satisfaction I got out of him was to be told that Thistle Plaster was not running. I said: 'What the hell are we waiting for, then?' He said: 'You're waiting here to see if they can get someone to change ower.' I said: 'Change ower. You get the doings off, lad. We want 10-15 out o'Carlisle. 'He said: 'It's cancelled.' I thought: 'There's summat funny here.' Eventually, he let us go. We pulled off—and away we went!

"We were making up for lost time. A train usually runs down in-to t'Eden Valey. In fact, you used to handbrake a little bit. But not that day, we didn't. 'Back signal' was on at Langwathby. As we were approaching t'outer, he popped a red flag out of t'window—which they did, for it was customary. He shoved his heeard out of t'window and said: 'You're swapping ower.' I said; 'Nivver'.

"Up the Pennine, down the Pennine; up the Pennine, down the Pennine—I thought, heck, we're going to have our money's worth. Anyway, fireman went potty. I said: 'Dont worry, lad; what thou can't do, I can.' Eventually, signalman said: 'He's coming now. When you've changed over, draw up to my up-starter and when the guards have changed over, I'll drop it, and then you can go.' I said: 'OK'.

"So when they come, I looked at Carlisle feller—A Durran Hillman—and I said: 'Eh up, there's summat funny here, owd lad.' He said: 'What?' I said: 'You should be lodging at Leeds, shouldn't you?' He said: 'Yes—but I'm afraid you haven't heard the news.' I said: 'News?' Only news I've heard is four pints for nowt in t'Club at dinner-time.' He said: 'The war's over. Victory over Japan's assured at last.' I said: 'Ohhhh—is there nowt running then?'

"He wanted to know how many trains I'd passed. I said: 'One—I think. And that were t'Scotch in the tunnil. It was a passenger o'some sort, anyway. 'He said: 'It'd bi t'Scotch. The other one's cancelled. All men working today must be lifted off and get into their own Control area. They'll get a day in lieu for working and they are in double pay'. I said: 'Eh—that's nice. I'd sooner have four bloody pints for nowt, though.'

"He said: 'All right. You've a chance to make history today in a No. 8. It'll be fully fitted with the exception of the first one, which was off at Hellifield. The vaccuum's been tried and the strings have been drawn, and you're running, until you require the ejector, with steam brake only.' I said: 'Oh, reighto—how'm I fixed for watter?' He said: 'I'm afraid you'll have to stop at Appleby. I don't think you've got enough to reach the troughs.' That was bad.

"So we stopped at Appleby and we filled the tank up. I estimate I lost four minutes between Langwathby and Appleby. We were running under class B timings, which gave us 25 minutes from Appleby to Kirkby Stephen and you wanted 22 minutes from Kirkby Stephen to Aisgill. I took 25 minutes to Aisgill—all t'lot! I were shiftin'.

"You've summat on watching for Garsdale's distant. And whether there's owt on t'railway or there isn't, you've got to watch 'em. Eventually I spotted it. And instead of letting 'em run, like they did do, the regulator came open again . . . and that was that! We did from Aisgill to Settle Junction in record time.

"I kept looking back at t'guard's brake. It were wobbling about. He couldn't do owt. He could only put his own brake on. He hadn't got t'vacuum brake. He couldn't stop us. I estimated that at various places on the roadway I was doing 85 miles an hour, which was illegal. Those men who can confirm what I did are dead now. One was t'driver who relieved me. And t'other man was his fireman. (It was t'fireman who made the remark: 'By gum, lad— you've travelled! At each signal box that you've past, chap said: 'This is him!' and next minute you'd gone!').

"Relief driver said: 'I was sorry to come away misself. But if it's any consolation, I shall be relieved as soon as we get in t'Leeds area, and t'first, most expeditious way home will be mine. Even if I have to get on a bus!'

"As for me, that VJ Day ride was the best trip I ever had . . ."

Overleaf: Laying the tramway from Batty Green to Blea Moor.